Joe Knable speaks to the issue of the [barcode obscures text] *with resolution, clarity, truthfulness, and a noncompromising attitude. I believe this book can be a blessing and a plumb line for any young man who wants to keep his way pure by "keeping his way according to God's word."*

Tommy Nelson
Pastor, Denton Bible Church

Joe Knable doesn't write like a theologian-general sitting high above the battle but as a soldier right in the middle of the fight. His approach is straightforward, unashamed, humorous and, most importantly, biblical. Chock-full of stories and examples, Joe rocks the world of every young man's journey through the battle of lust and sex giving sane, practical, and not always comfortable, advice.

Dr. Bill Brown
President, Cedarville University

Joe takes a bold stance against sexual sin with an arsenal of Scripture and testimonies. Sexual sin is severely crippling the spiritual health of young men across our nation, and this book faces the tough issues without apology. As a college student, the book hit me right where I was standing, challenging me to take an aggressive stance against this very real, very dangerous problem.

Jeff Mitchell, 21 Years Old

It has been my privilege to know Joe Knable for the past four years. I know Joe as a man of honor and purity. This book is a result of his passion for the Word of God and his implementation of spiritual disciplines necessary to his and every man's holiness. I recommend Joe's book and pray that God will use it to reach men of all ages for His glory.

Dr. Paul Dixon
Chancellor of Cedarville University

Sex and the Single Guy *is a valuable resource in fighting the pandemic of sexual immorality that has overtaken our culture. Joe writes as a single guy, one who is in the battle in real-time, and this creates a relevance and immediacy that is hard to find in other books. His raw, truthful, and biblical insights on the subject will prove essential to any man wanting to live the pure and wonderful life that God desires us to enjoy. The truth will most certainly set you free, and Joe has provided an arsenal of truth for the single guy in these powerful pages. Biblical, and full of grace and truth; this is a valuable resource for every guy's library.*

Bob Gresh
Author of *Who Moved the Goalpost?* and
cofounder of Pure Freedom ministries

Fight fire with fire! Joseph Knable's honest work will get your mind in gear for your personal war for purity. Just saying "no" will never be enough—learn how to move from defense to offense in your battle against lust. Life doesn't go anywhere good until you actively take hold of God's power for your holiness.

Dr. James MacDonald, Senior Pastor of Harvest Bible Chapel
Radio Bible teacher, *Walk in the Word*

Direct, biblical, and practical are words that describe Sex and the Single Guy. *Joe Knable gets to the heart of the matter without pulling punches. If you really want to get serious about winning the battle for purity, this book is for you. Give copies to your friends as well. I highly recommend it.*

Pastor Bob Rohm
V.P. Christian Ministries, Cedarville University

Sex and the Single Guy: Winning Your Battle for Purity *sets itself apart as a live, on scene journal, penned from a foot solider in a life or death fight to preserve God's holiness in his sex life. From confession to victory, Joe's timely and transparent testimony extolled, encouraged, and equipped me to rejuvenate my obedience to God's Word and fight a pure fight.*

Chris Lucarini, Age 24

In his book, Joe contends that every single man can win the war against sexual impurity through God's enabling grace. Joe reiterates the timeless truths of Scripture, which are pertinent to every male struggling to please God with his sexuality. His cry is that we walk in the Spirit in our personal lives, and thereby embrace the abundant life that Christ longs to give each of us. In my relationship with Joe, I have found a man whose life corresponds with the difficult, yet liberating words found in the pages of this book.

Mark Awabdy, 22 Years Old

Sex and the Single Guy

WINNING YOUR BATTLE FOR PURITY

Joseph Knable

MOODY PUBLISHERS
CHICAGO

All Scripture quotations, unless otherwise indicated, are taken from the *Holy Bible, New International Version*®. NIV®. Copyright © 1973, 1978, 1984 by International Bible Society. Used by permission of Zondervan Publishing House. All rights reserved.

Scripture quotations marked NLT are taken from the *Holy Bible, New Living Translation,* copyright © 1996. Used by permission of Tyndale House Publishers, Inc., Wheaton, Illinois 60189, U.S.A. All rights reserved.

Scripture quotations marked KJV are taken from the King James Version.

Library of Congress Cataloging-in-Publication Data

Knable, Joseph.
    Sex and the single guy : winning your battle for purity / Joseph Knable.
       p. cm.
    Includes bibliographical references.
    ISBN-13: 978-0-8024-9204-3
      1. Chastity. 2. Christian men—Sexual behavior. 3. Single people—Sexual behavior. 4. Sex—Religious aspects—Christianity. 5. Sexual ethics. I. Title.

BV4647.C5K56 2005
241'.66--dc22

                                  2004028342

ISBN: 0-8024-9204-5
EAN/ISBN-13: 978-0-8024-9204-3

1 3 5 7 9 10 8 6 4 2

Printed in the United States of America

For all my fellow warriors.
May you be inspired and equipped
to live a victorious and joyful life of fruitful service
to our Lord Jesus.

Contents

Foreword

W H E N was the last time you had a sexual thought? Be honest! Five hours ago? Five minutes ago? Five seconds ago? Let me ask you another question: Why is that a subject thought about so often yet addressed so sparingly from a godly, biblical perspective?

My friend Joe Knable has pondered this question, and taken action. You hold in your hand the product of his passion. Unlike other books on this topic, this book is written by a single guy for single guys. He fights in the trenches of this battle right beside you as he writes, transparently recalling his failures, sharing his intense struggle for victory, and highlighting the life-transforming power of God's grace through it all.

Sex and the Single Guy

Sex and the Single Guy is brutally honest, and doesn't candy coat or tiptoe around topics such as lustful thoughts, pornography, and masturbation. With an *effective* and *captivating* combination of humor, personal stories, practical advice, and even a section written by ladies lending insights that men rarely think about, this book will challenge you to rise above mediocrity and equip you for battle. Bringing God's Word to bear on the issue of sexual purity, it points to the undeniable fact that we are in a war for our very souls!

In my years as a youth and college pastor, I have personally witnessed many casualties of this war. It breaks my heart every time I see promising young men caught in the snare that Satan has set. Our enemy has made it his business to sabotage the wonderful God-given gift of sexuality, turning it into a trap that keeps guys from fulfilling their mission as disciplined soldiers for Christ.

My brothers, if you are serious about fighting and winning the battle for your sexual purity, then this book is for you. Perhaps you've failed a thousand times and feel like a prisoner of war. Read on and you will see that you are not alone and that there is hope.

God can set you free. Don't run and hide like a coward in this war. By the grace of God, and the power of His Spirit, take a stand and fight! Your soul is at stake!

MARK IRVING
Director of Discipleship Ministries,
Cedarville University
Conference Speaker

Acknowledgments

T O Sam Richard, Joe Schneider, Andy Jenkins, Ben Sprague, Stephen Bauer, Brad Smith, Jim Amstutz, and everyone else who has kept me accountable over the years: Thank you. I wouldn't have made it without you.

I am also grateful to those who have mentored me and taught me what it is to be a true follower of Christ through the years, especially Uncle Rick, Uncle Tim, David Life, Pastor Bob Hudberg, Pastor Bob Rohm, Lt. Col. Bert Fujishige, Dr. Bill Brown, and Pastor Phil Waters. Thank you for sticking with me as I grew.

Thanks also to all my friends who contributed to this project and encouraged me or prayed for me along the way, especially Chris Lucarini, Jeff Mitchell, Mark Awabdy,

Jared Honeycutt, Dr. Scott Calhoun, and all the guys and girls whose stories have brought this book to life.

A talented team at Moody Publishers helped make this book a reality. In particular, I'm grateful for the vision and work of Greg Thornton, Betsey Newenhuyse, Karen Waddles, and Jim Vincent.

A special thank-you goes to Pastor Alistair Begg for seeing the potential in this message and for making all of this possible.

Finally, to my Lord and Savior, Jesus Christ: This is Your message, Your ministry, and I am Your grateful servant. May You be glorified by this book.

" Purity is the outcome of sustained spiritual sympathy with God. We have to grow in purity . . . The only thing that safeguards is the Redemption of Jesus Christ. If I will hand myself over to Him, I need never experience the terrible possibilities that are in my heart. Purity is too deep down for me to get to naturally: but when the Holy Spirit comes in, He brings into the center of my personal life the very Spirit that was manifested in the life of Jesus Christ, . . . which is unsullied purity.

OSWALD CHAMBERS
My Utmost for His Highest

Finally, brothers, whatever is true, whatever is noble, whatever is right, whatever is pure, whatever is lovely, whatever is admirable—if anything is excellent or praiseworthy—think about such things.

Philippians 4:8

CHAPTER 1

From One Guy to Another

MARK sat at his favorite table at Montevoni's and didn't wait long before his favorite waitress arrived.

"Hi, Mark! How are you?"

"Oh, hi, Theresa. It's been a while, hasn't it? I haven't seen you in here the last couple of weeks."

"Oh, classes have been busy, so I had to take some time off from work. It's hard to concentrate on waiting tables when you have four big exams to study for."

"Oh, I understand! I've been there. I miss college a lot, but not those exams." *Man, she looks really nice today. I've never noticed how attractive she is.*

"So how is work, Mark? Has anything happened since the last time we talked?"

"No, it's just been another busy, stressful week. How about you?" *Why haven't I ever asked her out before? She's nice, she's really cute, and she's a solid Christian girl. I should ask her out sometime.*

"It's been good, but it can get pretty old sometimes. But it's a great job to help put me through college."

"I'm sure it would be—I worked as a waiter for a couple of years when I was in college." *You know, I really like this girl.*

"Yeah, I like it because they work with my class schedule, and the customers are so nice."

That's because her shirt is so tight. Does she have any idea what that shirt does to me? Those pants are also too tight . . . but I don't really mind. "Oh, that's just because you're such a nice girl."

"Yeah, right. So how is your family, Mark? Did your sister get engaged yet?"

"No. We thought he was going to ask her last weekend when they went up to see my parents, but her boyfriend chickened out." *Wow, she has some great curves.* "I'm sure it will be any time now. How is your family doing?"

It was a slow Wednesday, so Theresa was taking more time to chat than she normally would. Mark liked that.

"Everybody is OK, except my dad," she said. "He went in for a routine physical last Tuesday, and the tests found something, and now he needs to go to see a specialist about it. It's kind of scary."

"I'm really sorry to hear about that." *Do you honestly know how hot you are?*

"We think he's gonna be OK, but he was really tired and stayed in bed all week."

"That's not any fun at all. I had to stay in bed for a week last summer when I had mono; I couldn't do anything but watch TV." *However, I wouldn't mind being stuck in bed with you for a week.*

"As soon as I get off work I need to go check up on him."

"That's really cool of you; I admire how much you care about your dad." *I wonder what she'd let me do with her on our first date.*

"It's the least I can do for the guy who's always done so much for me."

"My dad's the same way . . . Hey listen, Theresa, I know it's difficult, but don't forget that God is in control of this. Even if they do find something, God already knows about it, and there's nothing too difficult for Him to handle." *Man, I'd like to handle her. If we could have just five minutes alone . . .*

"You're absolutely right, Mark. I just need to trust God with this. It's hard sometimes, but I do trust Him."

"Good to hear. Hey, I need to get going; I need to be back to work by one."

"Well, thanks for the encouragement, Mark. I really needed it. I'm glad I got to see you today. We should talk like this more often."

I'll tell you what we should do more often . . . "You too, Theresa. Hey, I'll be praying for your dad, OK?" *I just want to take you and . . .*

"Thanks, Mark; God bless you."

"See ya later, Theresa." *Do you know what I'd like to do? Man, I wish I could take you to the backseat of my car right now . . . Wait—what am I doing? What in the world is wrong with me? God, please help me!*

Welcome to the Battlefield

We have a big problem, and it's affecting every one of us. It's even destroying some of us. The problem is sexual sin. Every day this battle is taking out more guys, and it's holding even more guys back. Why shouldn't it be you or me? What makes us any different than any one of them? Better men than us have fallen.

Those outside the Christian church sit back and scoff as Christian guys fall into immorality as rampantly as they do. Who will take a stand and show them that the power God has given us over sin is real, and the change He's made in our lives is lasting?

If you are a follower of Jesus, you know the Good News: On the cross, Christ took the penalty of sin for us. When we were born again, Christ killed in us the lordship that sin had over us. Sin is no longer our master. Yet so many times we serve it still. Why do we do that, and what can we do about it? If you truly want to know answers to those questions—and especially how to overcome bondage to sexual sin—then you've come to the right place.

Sex and the Single Guy is no substitute for Scripture—although the message is born of and subordinate to the Word of God, and driven by the undeniably real and lasting work that our mighty God has done in many lives, including my own. This book features the thoughts about seventy guys, twenty women, and thirty books and resources. It explores why we guys do what we do, how we can live a transformed life, and all that awaits us when we do.

Allow Me to Introduce Myself

My name is Joe Knable, and I'm an unmarried fourth-year college student at Cedarville University in Ohio. You might be wondering why you should listen to a "kid" like me. I'm writing because I have an intense passion for sexual purity and holiness, as well as a personal vendetta against sexual sin. You might be interested in hearing what

I have to say because I *am* a young, unmarried guy just like you.

You see, almost every hard-hitting resource on sexual purity for guys that I have come across has been written by a married man. A lot of single guys might have some difficulty receiving counsel from these married guys in this area. When it comes to sexual purity, we're talking about two totally different worlds. They're striving for *fidelity,* while we're striving for *abstinence!*

After reading a myriad of articles and books from married men sharing their stories of victory after many devastating years of failure, it makes you wonder if true sexual purity is something that we may only achieve after marriage. Well, my friend, that is not true! Purity, holiness, and integrity are things that we single guys can know and live today, here and now! God has blessed me with this reality, and with all my heart I want you to experience it as well. Here's just a taste of my story, which I will tell in more detail later on.

All of my adolescent life I struggled with sexual sin, including lust and masturbation, and sometimes even pornography and physical encounters with girls. This sin racked my mind and my heart daily and would manifest itself in devastating ways in my life, the worst of which was a marred relationship with my Savior, Jesus Christ.

I tried a thousand different approaches to tackle this sin, but nothing worked. Then one day I became fed up with it, but rather than myself, I turned to the Word of God for the answer. What I found was a bountiful feast of Scripture that spoke directly to my struggles! I applied verses like Psalm 119:9 and 11 and 2 Timothy 2:22 to my life.

Thus, on August 3, 2002, I declared war on this sexual

sin, relying on Christ for strength and direction. What I experienced from that time on was the most amazing and real victory I have ever known in my life.

Please understand that I haven't somehow become immune to temptation. In fact, the struggle with sexual temptation continues every day. The victory is that the *trend* of my life is radically different from what it was before. God has changed my attitude and perspective toward sin and holiness dramatically. This is all about the Lord Jesus Christ and the life-changing power He wields over sin, which is communicated to us through His Holy Word. I will tell my story in more detail in chapter 2, but first we need to define this struggle a little more clearly.

Your Problem—and Mine

I don't think there's any secret to why lust appeals to us. We're guys, we have raging hormones and God-given sex drives, and we're single. What do we do?

Well, a lot of us indulge those hormones. Some guys like to watch trashy television or movies; other guys have an uncontrollable addiction to Internet pornography. Some guys get a fix from going places to just sit and watch and mentally devour the women that walk by, and they store up all of those thoughts and images for that night when they will lie alone someplace and masturbate. There are also guys who engage in regular sex with their girlfriends—or other girls they're not even committed to. Or maybe they never go all the way, but they do things with women that make either themselves or the women think sexual thoughts.

Is there anything wrong with expressing ourselves sexually in these ways, as long as we're willing to accept the consequences? There is if we appeal to God's standard.

Here's the measuring stick the Bible has set up for us when it comes to purity: "But among you there must not be even a hint of sexual immorality, or of any kind of impurity" (Ephesians 5:3).

How do we define "sexual immorality"? Jesus Himself did that in Matthew 5:28: "Anyone who looks lustfully at a woman has already committed adultery with her in his heart." All of these expressions of our sexual cravings—fornication, viewing pornography, doing anything to stir up thoughts of lust, and even masturbation—hinge on the foundation of lustful thoughts. Jesus equates lust with adultery, which is punishable by death in the Old Testament (Leviticus 20:10) and is listed right after murder in the New Testament (Matthew 5:21–22, 27–28).

It's important to clarify what lust is and what it is not. You and I and most other guys are attracted to pretty girls. There's nothing wrong with attraction; without it, you and I would have never been born. And there's much more to our sexual attraction than just mere procreation; God is the author of attraction and the mastermind behind romance, and He delights when we enjoy these blessings in the manner He intended. But sin is looking at that pretty girl in an unholy way, thinking sexual thoughts about her, or even just dwelling on a desire for her. John Eldredge explains how attraction can quickly turn to lust that is sinful and destructive:

> You'll see a beautiful woman and something in you will say, *You want her.* That's the Evil One appealing to the traitor within. If the traitor says, *Yes, I do,* then the lust really begins to take hold. Let that go on for years and you've given him a stronghold.[1]

So this is why we're here. We have a giant sin problem, and it's affecting every area of our life. If you're brave enough, and if you care enough, then join me as we wrestle through these issues together and find out what we can do to fight our lust and bring our sexual feelings under control, by the power of God and the instruction of His Word.

The Best Sex Imaginable

I am not against sex. I thought it might be important to make that clarification at this point, in case you were beginning to wonder. Sex is a precious gift from God, and it is something that He intended for us to enjoy heartily. The consensus from the married couples I know is that they do enjoy it, very much.

There is a catch, however. The act of sex is not a gift that we can use any time we want, with whomever we want. There are strict boundaries for how the blessing of sex is to be enjoyed, and they are carefully laid out in the Bible. Sex is something that is to be enjoyed by a man and a woman only after they are married. To experience sex in any other context would be to taint God's intention for the blessing. In other words, it just wouldn't be as good. It would be a tragic, lost opportunity for your sexual fulfillment, and a perversion of God's gift of sex.

Sex outside of marriage involves loss of self-control, carnal lust, selfishness, deceit, and a whole host of other destructive behaviors. Its effects can be devastating: broken hearts; broken homes; broken relationships with family members, friends, and the Lord Jesus; and physical consequences such as unwanted pregnancies and sexually transmitted diseases, including AIDS.

Would you like to have a successful marriage someday? So would I. I have talked to countless couples, pastors, and counselors, and they agree unanimously that having sex outside of marriage, even fornication committed in the past before the spouses met, makes that marriage much more difficult. This isn't to say that someone who has had sex outside of marriage could never have a successful marriage; with God, all things are possible. It only means that they have another hurdle to overcome on the way to marital success.

Sex is a beautiful thing, but we have to keep it in context. Allow me to illustrate this point further.

Chainsaws and Dental Floss

Sex is like a chainsaw. A chainsaw in its place is a great tool; it can be used to cut down trees and turn them into manageable slabs of wood we can turn into firewood or lumber. You wouldn't use a chainsaw to floss your teeth, however. Sex inside of marriage is like a chainsaw in a forest: It belongs. Sex outside of marriage brings the chainsaw into the bathroom, where it doesn't belong and where it might get awfully messy. You get the point; sex outside of marriage messes up a great thing that God has given us, and the results are devastating. Sex is awesome—we just need to play by the rules.[2]

Fighting Back

Girls will always be attractive, and we will always be tempted to look at them lustfully. What I do contend, however, is that we can learn to *choose purity* each time—to regard and respect them as beautiful creations. How do we do this? If we are saved by Jesus' sacrifice, we have the Spirit of the living God living inside of us. We are saved from slavery to sin. No longer slaves, we have a choice. From the Word of God we can learn how we choose purity: "You have been set free from sin and have become slaves to righteousness" (Romans 6:18).

It doesn't matter how much you struggle with pornography, how many girls you have slept with, or how often or how long you have been masturbating; you can have victory in Jesus! "Who shall separate us from the love of Christ?" (Romans 8:35). God has changed my life with the lessons He has taught me through His Word, and He wants to give you victory over sexual sin as well.

Don't underestimate our God. He can do it. Please read on and share the rest of this message with me, believing all the while that "I can do everything through him who gives me strength" (Philippians 4:13).

REFLECTIONS

"Reflections" concludes each chapter with questions or activities to help you bring the principles from the chapter home. Use these items for personal reflection, as part of a group study, or in a meeting with a trusted friend or mentor who will hold you accountable in your spiritual walk.

1. *What are your thoughts on the issue of sexual sin? What actions or thoughts do you think incorporate sexual sin? What is your definition of lust?*

2. *What do you hope to get out of reading this book? Write down three to five personal goals now, and look back at them when you're finished.*

" When men are troubled with the guilt of a sin that has prevailed over them, they promise themselves and God that they will sin thus no more, but they seek to accomplish their own victory. They watch over themselves and pray for a short season until the pain of conviction waxes cold and the sense of sin wears off. Mortification then also goes to the door, and sin returns to its former dominion.

JOHN OWEN
The Mortification of Sin

Dear friends, I urge you, as aliens and strangers in the world, to abstain from sinful desires, which **war** *against your soul.*

1 Peter 2:11 (emphasis added)

CHAPTER 2

War Has Been Declared!

I DON'T think I'll ever forget that terrible day the war began. I was eleven years old, and I had recently started to feel the full effects of this strange period of life called puberty. As I recall, it was marvelous and terrible at the same time.

I was younger than most of my friends, so I learned about the "M word" earlier than other guys would. My friend Ted (except where full names are given, all names have been changed) and I were on the same football team, and after practice we went over to his house like we often did. Most of the time we played video games or watched TV, but on this particular day, we just hung out and talked.

The subject of girls was brought up, and how "hot" so

many of them at school were becoming. Then Ted told me about something that sounded really weird. He said he knew how to masturbate, and it was really fun. You felt strong and strange at the same time, and you got hot inside, he said. That sounded weird all right, but also exciting. It was all I could think about that day, and when I went home that night and I was alone in my room, I thought about all the girls I had stared at that day. (Later I would learn this was lust.) Then I began to do to myself what Ted described. It was really weird and exciting, and it felt really bad all at the same time.

"The Sex Talk"

You may be reading this and wondering, *Why was Ted the only one to tell you about these things? Why were you alone with your friends and your own thoughts?* Well, I have often wondered the same thing.

I suspect my sex talk was one of the shortest sex talks in recorded adolescent history. Here goes: At around the same time the above event took place, my dad and I were driving around in his great big blue 1976 Chevy Impala. That thing had a huge engine and my dad was always tweaking it and souping it up to make it more powerful. It was a classic. My dad seemed to be in deep thought, and he wasn't saying anything. We stopped at a stoplight, and my dad, with both hands firmly on the steering wheel, looked over at me and said sharply and seriously: "Boy, don't ever get a girl pregnant. It'll ruin your life." Then the light turned green, and he peeled off.

That was it.

Amazing! Wow, that really gave me some moral direction. He told me nothing about sex, nothing about marriage, and, most important, he told me nothing about all of these new sexual thoughts and feelings I was experiencing. To this day, I've never heard him mention the "M word" or anything like it.

It wasn't just my dad who was silent, however. I didn't hear anything about it from my pastor at church, my teachers at school, or any adults, for that matter. The only information I was taking in regarding this issue was from sex-driven TV shows, movies, other media, and my hormone-driven friends. Even so, I heard a still, small voice in my heart convicting me that lust and masturbation were wrong.

The Struggle Continues

In the next eight years I did many of the same things that any adolescent boy does. I went to school and church, played football, visited my aunts and uncles on Christmas and Thanksgiving, went to the movies, and got my driver's license. Through it all, however, there was something that always hung over me. It was sexual sin. I started masturbating when I was eleven, and it only got worse as the years went by. It was something that all of the guys in the locker room admitted to, and they created a rule that you were only weird if you didn't do it. It was always something I felt dirty and convicted about, but that didn't stop me.

I would go through the day staring as much as I could get away with at the girls who wore anything that invited lustful thoughts. At a public junior high and high school, that is not very tough to do! I didn't want to masturbate, but at the end of the day I had fed my hormones with the lustful thoughts of girls so much that I thought I just couldn't help it.

At age fifteen I gave my life to Jesus. I was so excited about Christ that I didn't masturbate for about four months.

Sadly, that didn't last, and I continued to struggle for another four years just like I had before. God changed my life in many ways. His redeeming power was very evident in my life, but I continued to act enslaved by the lust of the flesh and its sinful fulfillment.

I think I tried just about everything to get rid of the sin throughout the years. I would cry out to God . . . make declarations that *today* would be the day it would end . . . and do all sorts of other crazy things to try to rid myself of the battle. I was on my own the whole time. It's a wonder that a boy is allowed to do something so wrong for so long without getting in trouble for it. Why must adults stay so silent when it comes to this issue?

Although I was never confronted or punished by my parents or any other person for this, God seemed to chastise me for it constantly. I knew some of the basic elements of why I sinned like this, such as the main reason I fell into masturbation at night when I didn't want to was because I built up so much sexual tension by the lustful looks I'd taken all day long. This knowledge allowed me to go for a few days or a week here and there without masturbating, as I tried to look much less or told myself, *You only want to do this because you stared at those girls too much.* Occasionally there would even be a few weeks when I really tried hard and didn't fall, but my efforts were really quite feeble.

This sin was crippling my walk with the Lord. In the years that followed my salvation, my walk was very sweet, and I became very active in junior high youth ministry and evangelism, and Bible studies at school. Still, I don't think I ever reached my full potential because of this struggle.

Through these years, I never thought that God was correcting me without a purpose. Long before I even liked girls I dreamed of having a loving, godly family. Even as a young boy I felt the Lord saying to me, "Joe, you need to learn faithfulness to Me in this if you think that you are ever going to be faithful as a husband or a father. If you can't follow Me in this area, what makes you think that I would ever trust you with something so precious as a wife or children to care for?" God is faithful, and eight years after the struggle began, He changed my life in such a tremendous way by giving me tools to overcome this struggle.

My Turning Point

On August 3, 2002, I declared war. I awoke that morning feeling fed up with my struggle over sexual sin. I decided that I was going to run after God until I got some solid, tangible answers about how to find victory. I gave up all my other plans for the day and spent the entire day in the Word, in prayer, and in my journal, seeking God on this matter:

> "Dear friends, I urge you, as aliens and strangers in the world, to abstain from sinful desires, which WAR against you soul" (1 Peter 2:11). . . .

> I'm done. I hate sin, especially sexual sin, and I especially hate what it does to my relationship with my Savior. God has called me as His son, and He has spent special attention rebuking me regarding this particular sin (Hebrews 12:4-6). I can't claim to know the intricate plans or ways of God, but I might venture some guesses to this—perhaps it is His plan to give me a wife someday and children—and it is imperative that I conquer this challenge in order that I may learn to be faithful to them. For if I am unfaithful in the small things, what makes me think I'll be faithful in the big things (Nehemiah 7:2)? I love my wife and kids already, whoever they are, and so I desire to learn faithfulness for their sake, but I love Christ Jesus my Lord even more—my Lord who has made every effort to make me like Him.

>>

That's how my journal entry began on August 3. But there was much more, reflecting frustration, determination, and a solid plan for fighting back. Here are some excerpts from the entry, which was entitled "War Has Been Declared":

"I do not understand what I do. For what I want to do I do not do.... For I have the desire to do what is good, but I cannot carry it out. For what I do is not the good I want to do; no, the evil I do not want to do—this I keep on doing.... For in my inner being I delight in God's law; but I see another law at work in the members of my body, WAGING WAR against the law of my mind and making me a prisoner of the law of sin at work within my members. What a wretched man I am!" (Romans 7:15, 18–24).

I couldn't have said it better myself. And I've come at this at 300 different angles. I've said so many things to God. But a few things I've observed: 1. I'm never idle! I'm either running after Christ Jesus, or running after my lustful passion. 2. Jesus was never idle either! He was *always* running after His Father's will and the purpose for which He had come to earth. So then, perhaps I should acknowledge that I've been spared from God's wrath, and then I should run forever after the purpose for which I've been spared. The first is that God would have one more genuine worshiper—so I must make that by itself my primary objective. The second is to share His grace with the fallen world. For this, I must set aside my selfish ambition, shoulder my cross, put on the full armor of God, and follow Jesus in His never-ceasing ministry (Matthew 16:24; Ephesians 6:10–18).

But this is not all of it.... All this time I've been searching and longing for the *solution*: the easy answer that will rid me of this devastating struggle and make me forever perfectly pure. But I forget who I am and where I am! I am a fallible human being, born into and forever inclined to sin, and I live in a sin-ridden world where the deceiver has established his kingdom and will reign until God deems it time for him to be banished forever. . . . My struggle remains until I die! (Or Christ comes.) So then, I must not view this problem as one where I'll find a magic spell and it will be cured, but rather as a WAR that must rage on until the time Christ Jesus comes in all of His Glory to establish His kingdom here on earth. WAR HAS BEEN DECLARED THIS DAY, and thanks be to God, for GREATER IS HE THAT IS IN ME THAN he THAT IS IN THE WORLD! (1 John 4:4). . . .

To survive, and to WIN, I must daily tap into the source—I must hide God's Word in my heart (Psalm 119:9, 11) and put on the whole armor of God (Ephesians 6). What comes out of my mouth and my life will depend on what I put into them. If I feed myself filth from TV, movies, conversations, then filth will come out. But if I feed on God's Word and godly things, then these same things will be produced in my life.

I must never expect to be immune to temptation (1 Corinthians 10:12). I will always be susceptible! God's provision comes [when during the temptation] "he will also provide a way out, so that you can STAND UP under it" [see verse 13]. So this war is going to be a trial-by-trial, situation-by-situation, temptation-by-temptation thing. . . .

As each temptation arises, I must check it against God's Word. I must "take every thought captive and make it obedient to Christ" (2 Corinthians 10:5). If I see something that stimulates my youthful lust, I must not dwell with it! I must RUN! If there's a magazine lying around, cover it up without taking a peek. If there's something on TV or a movie, then I must turn it off, leave the room, or avert my eyes without even giving it a second glance.

I must not even stick my toe in the door of sexual immorality. I want to see girls as God sees them—with absolute purity.

I know the things I must do to have victory; it's just that I must do them each time and never expect to be immune to the next temptation (1 Corinthians 10:12).

Praise God in the name of His Son Jesus for giving me these powerful words of wisdom and VICTORY!

Your word is a lamp to my feet and a light for my path.
— *Psalm 119:105*

Equipped for Battle

As I write this, it's been two years since that day when God changed my approach to fighting the war for purity. Now I use the truth of His Word. I certainly haven't gotten rid of this temptation, and I've sinned many times since then. But the change has been lasting, as I have fallen less in the past two and a half years than I might have in just two weeks beforehand. There's nothing exceptional about me that has enabled me to experience victory over this sin; I've just learned to fight a longstanding war that has been waged against me. I've learned that John Owen was right when he said, "Always be killing sin or sin will be killing you." I'm praying that this book, and more important the Scripture verses cited herein, will help equip you to fight and win each battle that comes your way as well. While you prayerfully work your way through the rest of this book, be sure to test each idea against the Word of God. As you continue, please pray with me:

"Lord Jesus, thank You for giving me life, and for giving me life again when I was lost in my sins. You have created me, and You have saved me from the fires of hell, so I know that there is nothing You cannot do. I am tired of living this life crippled by sexual sin. I hate the guilt it produces, and I especially hate the way it hinders my relationship with You. I know You have broken the power of death in my life, but sometimes I sure do feel like I still wear the chains when it comes to this. Rescue me from this body of death, O God! I know that You are able to show me how to have victory over this and any sin, so I ask in Your precious name that You would use this book and the Scripture You have already given me to do just that. Thank You so much. May I praise You as long as I live. Amen."

REFLECTIONS

1. *In what ways can you relate to the author's testimony regarding his struggles and triumphs over this sin?*

2. *What is your story in regard to sexual sin and purity? Write your own story thus far down in your journal or tell it to a friend whom you trust.*

> **“** The stench of sin is always foul; so then why do I breathe deeply and seek to taste its fruits?
>
> **CHRIS**
> *age twenty-two*

*When I want to do good, evil is right there with me. For in my inner being I delight in God's law; but I see another law at work in the members of my body, **waging war** against the law of my mind and making me a prisoner of the law of sin at work within my members. What a wretched man I am! Who will rescue me from this body of death?*

Romans 7: 21–24 (emphasis added)

CHAPTER 3

Why Do We Keep Sinning?

B I L L had been on a long bike ride. His friends were supposed to meet him in the next county, but they couldn't find him. There was no other mode of transportation available, so, alone with his bike, Bill had to find his way back. He needed to return to work the next day or he would lose his job at the video store. He got on his bike and started pedaling like mad.

He went mile after mile, through town after town. He got tired but kept going. Pedaling and pedaling, he passed cows and horses and cherry orchards. Before long only one word described every desire in his heart: *thirst.* He had gone over thirty miles by this time and hadn't had a sip of water. He was so terribly thirsty. Even a sip of warm, dirty water would have done at this point. But he pressed on, thinking about the cold, refreshing Snapples in the refrigerator in the back room of the video store.

Dying of Thirst

Fifty miles now, but Bill continued on. His vision started to blur, and he began to see mirages in the distance. "Oh look, a babbling brook!" he exclaimed, but no, it was just another cow. He considered the possibilities . . . but he wasn't *that* thirsty. On and on he rode, all the while wishing he had brought his own brand-new Mongoose bicycle instead of his eleven-year-old sister's Barbie bike with its great big basket.

Then suddenly he saw the first signs of his town. He was almost home!

"Snapple, here I come!" he shouted. But it was too late. His body was too dehydrated, and exhaustion overtook him, sending him crashing to the ground.

Some passersby saw Bill and called for an ambulance. When the EMTs arrived and looked at the cyclist's unconscious body, they discovered strapped to his back a Camel-Bak water bottle full of cool, refreshing water. He had it with him the whole time, but he never realized it, and it almost cost him his life.

This story sounds ridiculous, and it is. It might come as a surprise to many of us, then, to learn that we do this all the time. We're so thirsty spiritually, and yet we have a God who is ready to satisfy our thirst at a moment's notice, yet we don't even come to Him or listen to His Word! Even if we do, we don't apply it. Reading the life-giving Word of God and not doing what it says would be like Bill taking a sip of that water when he was so thirsty, swishing it around in his mouth, and then spitting it out for no good reason and continuing on, thirsty. I have acted this way on count-less occasions. Let us learn a lesson from our friend Bill; let's stick that tube in our mouth, drink, and be satisfied! God has provided all the resources we need.

After reading this bizarre story about Bill and his CamelBak, take another look at John 4:13–14, where Jesus is telling the woman at the well about the living water. "Everyone who drinks this water will be thirsty again, but whoever drinks the water I give him will never thirst. In-deed, the water I give him will become in him a spring of water welling up to eternal life."

Why do we keep sinning? Because we refuse to drink from the well.

Two Hands

A friend of mine, Dan Rasbach, offered an illustration of sin that I will never forget. Hold up your hands, palms up, he said. (Go ahead, do it. Oh, you have a book in your hand. OK, open them up as much as you can.) Imagine that in your left hand is sin, and in your right hand is God's righteousness and acts of holy living. You try to push the sin in your left hand away and cling to the things in your right hand because you feel that you should, and you might get in trouble otherwise, and God deserves your obe-dience, and you want to keep up your "Christian image" to those who know you as a Christian. That doesn't last, how-ever, because what you really want is in your left hand. Deep in your heart, you think that the sinful thing is more fun, and it will be more gratifying for you. That stuff promises to give you immediate pleasure—no waiting! *Come on, live a little; it's not so bad!* You fight this urge because of your convictions, but eventually you give in to the loudest desires of your heart.

You'll never defeat sin this way. Sooner or later, you'll keep coming back to that sin if it is what you desire the most. However, if you look at both hands—the sinful stuff on the left, and the godly stuff on the right—and you know that while the junk on the left may look appealing on the outside, it's really all rotten on the inside, then you may be on your way to genuine change. The junk on the left is no good, and it won't satisfy you in the long run. The stuff on the right side, on the other hand, is what will really satisfy you. It won't make you feel bad afterward, and the pleasure will be everlasting.

So with all your heart and with a brain full of wisdom, you cast the stuff in your left hand aside because you want nothing to do with it, and you embrace the stuff in your right hand, because it is what your heart really wants. When you make this decision about sin and righteousness, and you embrace godliness because you know it's better for you and it's what you want the most, then you will start having victory over many different sins.

Do you know that our God is a good God, and He wants the best for you? That doesn't mean that everything will always be easy and every decision you make for Christ will be fun, but it does mean that you will be much better off if you embrace what God has for you instead of what your sinful nature would entice you to do. Consider these words of Jesus: "The thief comes only to steal and kill and destroy; I have come that they might have life, and have it to the full" (John 10:10).

Why do we keep sinning? Because in our hearts we still desire the left hand more than the right.

It All Starts With . . .

When a seventeen-year-old senior in high school has sex with his girlfriend, or when a college sophomore looks at pornography, or when a twenty-five-year-old guy lies awake at night unable to sleep until he gives in and masturbates, that guy's struggle did not begin there. Neither did the sin. You see, those actions, as the most common expressions of our sinful, carnal nature, often make us overlook the countless times we let our mind wander into lust each day. I guarantee that any guy who falls into fornication, pornography, or masturbation has already fallen into lust again and again that day or that week, and he has built up this incredible sexual tension that he believes he must somehow release.

I don't mean to downplay the devastating effects that these three sins have in our lives. If these things are not repented of and taken to Christ to be overcome, they can ruin our relationships, including those with our future wives and kids, and they can ruin ministry opportunities, and eventually our lives. Instead, what I do mean is to have you take a more serious and sober look at the sin of lust. Jesus made it pretty clear in the Sermon on the Mount: "Anyone who looks at a woman lustfully has already committed adultery with her in his heart" (Matthew 5:28). Fornication is sin. So is lust. As for spiritual consequences, Jesus makes no distinction. The difference is in earthly consequences, but both sins grieve our Lord.

Many times I have cried out to God after I masturbated, bellowing, "Why did I just do that, Lord? I didn't want to do it, and I didn't want to let You down one more time! Why am I so weak, God?"

I speak as if the temptation to masturbate sneaked up on me late at night with no warning. Nonsense! The Holy Spirit of God had been telling me throughout the day not to look lustfully at those girls, or to look at that magazine ad so carnally, but I had done it anyway. I reasoned, *I'm not really sinning if I don't do anything physical.* Well, if one thing consistently leads to another, then that first thing is probably as bad as the other thing, isn't it?

When I realized these two truths—that lust is just as bad as the other things, and that it usually leads to those other things—I began to realize that eliminating lust might be a key part to eliminating the other things! Oh, it's great to run from fornication, pornography, and masturbation, and I plead with you to do so for as long as you live, but you're going to do yourself one incredibly huge favor if you decide to abstain from sin *way before* the opportunity for those things ever presents itself.

Look at the commitment that Job made to abstain from lust: "I made a covenant with my eyes not to look lustfully at a girl" (Job 31:1). If we will listen to Jesus and join Job by looking away whenever we see something or someone that can stimulate our youthful lust, we will make resisting and running from those other temptations much, much easier!

Significantly, the apostle Paul told the young Timothy to actively avoid lust: "Run from anything that stimulates youthful lust" (2 Timothy 2:22 NLT).

Why do we keep sinning? Because we shoot ourselves in the foot all day long and expect that we can run the race well that night.

Forsaking the Fear of the Lord

The issue goes deeper. This is something that I'm just getting the hang of myself. Why do we keep sinning when we've been saved by a holy God who loves us and has done everything in the world for us? More than anything else, because we don't fear the Lord.

This isn't a very popular teaching in modern Christianity.

"Fear God? The gracious, loving heavenly Father—are you crazy?" I've thought long and hard why so many sexual liberties have become commonplace in this wicked age, even among Christians. I've wondered what gives me the nerve to continue to sin against God myself, when I know how wonderful walking with Him is and how awful running from Him can be. How is this possible? Because I forget Whom I'm dealing with. We treat God like He's some wise, loving little *kid*—we enjoy all the blessings He can deliver, but we neglect to revere Him as the author of life and all creation—the Lord God Almighty.

The Scriptures remind us that we have an awesome, mighty God who should have our respect and obedience. Consider just three verses: "The fear of the LORD is the beginning of wisdom" (Psalm 111:10). "Now let the fear of the LORD be upon you. . . . You must serve faithfully and wholeheartedly in the fear of the LORD" (2 Chronicles 19:7, 9).

The Lord God is our Father, and He is our friend, but He's also the same God who struck Ananias and Sapphira dead in the New Testament for lying (Acts 5:1–11), and He's the same God who warns, "No immoral, impure or greedy person . . . has any inheritance in the kingdom of Christ and of God" (Ephesians 5:5). Yes, He is our friend, but He ought to make us a bit nervous as well. The phrase "The fear of the LORD" is used in the New International Version twenty-two times, and every time the phrase describes an instruction of something the people ought to have. Jesus Himself said it in Matthew 10:28: "Do not be afraid of those who kill the body but cannot kill the soul. Rather, be afraid of the One who can destroy both soul and body in hell."

If we're habitually sinning against God with a callous, unrepentant heart, we've forgotten just whom we're dealing with. Our God is not to be trifled with, and learning to fear

Him all over will stir up a revolution regarding the sin in our lives.

Why do we keep sinning? Because we treat Him like this:

Pathetic Conversations with God

"Oh, hey God. I'm just studying away here. Another late, late night. Got that big Anatomy and Physiology final tomorrow; it's supposed to be a killer, you know. Oh, right, you do know. By the way, you wouldn't mind helping me out with that, would you? I would really appreciate it.

"I'm just doing some research here on the computer. Technology is so cool today; I can look at all of these research databases right from my room, at three o'clock in the morning! I don't know what I'd do without the Internet. Boy, it sure is late, isn't it? If I'm not careful, this will turn into an all-nighter. I hate the day after an all-nighter. I've really worked hard studying for this one; I sure hope I do better than that last one; it was a bear!

"Hey, what's that? I'd better just take a look. Oh, wow! . . . Uhh, Jesus, I think you'd better go; this stuff is just boring and you probably don't care about it anyway. . . . I mean, I thought it was something else. I thought it had something to do with anatomy, so I had to check it out. OK, you're right; I know what it is, but so what? It's been a really late night, and I'm tired. More than that, I'm tired of fighting.

"Besides, you gave me this sex drive, didn't you? I can't believe you; you make me this way with all my hormones and everything, you tell me not to have sex with my girlfriend until we get married, which we won't be able to do until we graduate college in two more years, and now you're giving me this guilt trip about looking at these girls on the computer! How much sense does that make? It's not like they're innocent; they posed for these pictures and they earn a living because people look at them, so what's the harm?

"I've got to get some satisfaction somehow, so would you rather I look at this stuff for a little bit and relieve myself, when no one else knows about it and no one else will be hurt, or do you want me to have sex with my girlfriend and possibly get her pregnant? You wouldn't want that, would you? Oh, I know my body is your temple and I've been bought with a price and all that. I know that this stuff won't satisfy me in the long run and that following you is the only thing that can satisfy the needs of my heart, but I'm horny right now, so shut up, go away, and leave me alone! I'm gonna look at these naked women and masturbate tonight because right now it's the most important thing to me!

"Oh, by the way, I'm gonna want you to come back tomorrow morning and fix everything I screw up tonight, OK? Also, make it so there aren't any consequences, as long as I promise to feel really bad about it. But for now, leave me alone and let me enjoy this sin in privacy. Thanks."

REFLECTIONS

1. *How can you relate your own struggles to the illustrations I've shared?*

2. *What other things do you think contribute to your struggle? Make a list of reasons why you think you struggle.*

" There is nothing the world so wants as holy men. The cause of Christ is paralyzed because of sin—sin in believers ... It may be some hidden sin that keeps God from using us more. Let us be honest with God, and ask Him to search us and show us ourselves.

D. L. MOODY
The Home Work of D. L. Moody

Yet I hold this against you: You have forsaken your first love. Remember the height from which you have fallen! Repent and do the things you did at first.

Revelation 2:4–5

Those whom I love I rebuke and discipline. So be earnest, and repent.

Revelation 3:19

If you repent, I will restore you that you may serve me.

Jeremiah 15:19

CHAPTER 4

Broken and Made Whole

S O M E guys may be thinking, *Whoa, man, it's way too early for this repentance stuff! Shouldn't that be at the end of the book?* The purpose of this book is not to spend 90 percent of the time trying to convince you that we have a problem that must be dealt with, and then the last few pages dealing with it. We just don't have time for that. I'm writing to guys who, like me, already realize there is a massive problem in their lives, and want to get busy fighting it. I'm writing to guys who know there is a war being waged against them, and they are ready to wage that war right back at the enemy.

The first step to victory over sin is to get back to that intimate relationship with Christ we once had. Jesus Himself told us that we ought to repent regularly, as He included "Forgive us our debts, as we also have forgiven our debtors" in the Lord's Prayer (Matthew 6:12). Let's examine some principles and passages of Scripture that will shed some light on this issue.

Saved . . . from What?

Sin is terrible, and we must never make light of it. While the sin we commit as a believer is not going to send us to hell, we're still doing the thing that would have landed us in hell, and we're doing the thing that put Jesus on the cross. God is not happy about our sin at all, and we shouldn't be either. James tells us to "wash your hands, you sinners, and purify your hearts, you double-minded. Grieve, mourn, and wail. Change your laughter to mourning and your joy to gloom. Humble yourselves before the Lord, and he will lift you up" (James 4:8–10).

We need to be broken before God about the sin we've committed so we can get back into fellowship with our Maker, who loves us and empowers us to stand up against future temptations. Our heart needs to be like that of Job, who, confronted by a holy God, declared: "My ears had heard of you but now my eyes have seen you. Therefore I despise myself and repent in dust and ashes" (Job 42:5–6).

Let me challenge you with something very important, something that I have already genuinely challenged myself with: Have you ever thought about what would happen to you if God had not saved you by His mercy and grace? The Bible tells us we all would have gone to hell (2 Thessalonians 1:8–9). So many times we hear Christians say or sing, "Thank You, God, for saving me," yet they don't think about the implications. What have they been saved from?

In fact, I wonder if a lot of Christians even *believe* that they would have gone to hell if God had not saved them.

There's no doubt that without Jesus Christ I would have gone straight to hell when I died. This was another major turning point for me when I grasped this fact; it made me appreciate Jesus' sacrifice that much more. I challenge you today to think about this. Consider what would have happened to you if Jesus hadn't died on the cross for your sins; let the thought of His sacrifice fill your heart with praise and thanksgiving for what God has done for you.

When we realize all that Christ has saved us from, then we are more grateful that He saved us in the first place, and we are quicker to repent and restore fellowship. We will have a heart of thanksgiving like Job did, who confessed, "I sinned, and perverted what was right, but I did not get what I deserved. He redeemed my soul from going down to the pit, and I will live to enjoy the light" (Job 33:27–28).

Hating All Sin

In his 1656 masterpiece, *The Mortification of Sin,* John Owens cautioned about only focusing on one sinful struggle: "We must hate all sin, as sin, and not just that which troubles us." He explained that only turning from sin that particularly bothers us is hypocritical, because it shows that we are selfish; we're preoccupied with our own peace and well-being. Instead, we should abhor the presence of any sin in our lives, and we should be mortified by what that sin did and does to our Savior. Those are pure and proper motives for repentance, and they will cause us to repent and run from much more than mere sexual sin. We need to see sins like lust, pride, anger, envy, and apathy in the same light that we see our sexual immorality.

Jesus taught the same thing, when he explained in

Matthew 5 that lust is as grievous a sin as adultery. We don't get nearly as worked up about lust as we do adultery or fornication, however. Everyone lusts, we tell ourselves, so we pacify it and let it go. But God commands us to be holy, and He commands us to mortify lust and other sins we tolerate right along with the ones that cause us unrest.

God is brilliant; He gave us this perspective to teach us holiness, but He is also looking out for our best interest. No one ever committed adultery without first committing lust. *If we don't lust, we won't commit adultery, either!* If we tolerate lust, we give sin a foot in the door and we make it easy for sin to break in and ruin our lives. But if we treat lust like it's the worst thing that it could become by repenting and mortifying it, then it won't be given the opportunity to go any further.

Guilt Is Not the Problem

We can't talk about sin without talking about guilt. I have read books and articles telling us to pacify guilt and simply ignore it (see, for example, *Every Young Man's Battle,* by Stephen Arterburn).[1] The argument against feeling guilt is that guilt merely pushes the guy further and further into the sin, so it must be useless. Here's what happens: A guy masturbates or looks at pornography (or both), and he feels terrible about it. He cannot look his female friends in the eye, and he feels ashamed everywhere he goes. He feels like pond scum. An empty void develops in his heart, and it eats away at him until he does something about it. He feels lonely, so he goes back to the pornography or masturbation for a sense of satisfaction and gratification again, only to start the whole awful process all over.

Writers who decry feelings of guilt are right in identifying the problem of this vicious cycle, but they miss the mark when they attempt to solve it by simply saying, "Keep the shame away."[2] How do we reconcile "Keep the shame away" with "Grieve, mourn, and wail. Change your laughter to mourning and your joy to gloom" in James 4:9? Remember Peter and the rooster? He certainly experienced some feelings of guilt and shame when he denied Jesus three times and when Jesus looked him straight in the eye afterward.

The sins that we commit *are* really bad, and we must not slap Jesus in the face by saying they really aren't all that bad. Did Jesus go to Calvary for sin that is not rotten enough to move us to tears? There is a real, proper sense of guilt we should feel.

Amazing Grace

Yet, with all this guilt, there is a solution that reconciles both how James and others tell us to feel about our sin with all that Jesus did for us on the cross. The solution: *grace!* The problem is not that we have too lofty a view of sin, but rather, that we have too meager a view of grace! Sin is terrible and was bad enough to send us to hell, but we must realize that the power of the blood of Christ is *greater* than the power of sin! The old hymn got it right: "Grace, grace, God's grace, grace that will pardon and cleanse within. Grace, grace, God's grace, grace that is greater than all our sin."[3]

Dear brother, do you know just how wonderful and powerful the grace of God is? I'm getting goose bumps right now just thinking about it. We must understand and believe how completely and sufficiently the Lord Jesus Christ removes these sins by the power of His blood, instantly and forever. As the Lord told the people of Israel, "Though your sins are like scarlet, they shall be as white as snow" (Isaiah 1:18).

We must never mistake the seriousness of sin, and we must also never make light of the awesome power of God's grace. These two truths combined should bend our heart toward genuine repentance.

Now that we have reconciled this issue, let us examine a few passages of Scripture that will guide us in repentance.

Three Psalms That Model Revival in Action

I discovered the impact of a trio of psalms a number of months ago: 38–40. The psalms show powerfully the journey in the heart of King David. He begins in Psalm 38 broken and prostrate before God (as in Psalm 51). "My guilt has overwhelmed me like a burden too heavy to bear," David cries. "I confess my iniquity; I am troubled by my sin" (38:4, 18).

I appreciate so much the honesty of what comes next. He finishes Psalm 38 with a plea for the Lord to come to him: "Come quickly to help me, O Lord my Savior" (verse 22). In Psalm 39, however, there is a delay. Oh, how I can relate to this—and maybe you can too. The peace of God does not always come in like a flood the second we come to Him in repentance. It always does eventually, but not always right away. David is not yet restored, and he patiently waits for the Lord.

Finally, in Psalm 40, we see the payoff. "I waited patiently for the LORD; he turned to me and heard my cry. He lifted me out of the slimy pit, out of the mud and mire; he set my feet on a rock and gave me a firm place to stand. He put a new song in my mouth, a hymn of praise to God."

Go ahead and read it right now in your Bible; it's too long for me to include all of it here. Oh, God is good, and He is so incredibly faithful! When we repent, let us wait on the Lord and know that He *is* going to come to us and restore us to sweet fellowship with Him.

The Prodigal Son: Undeserved Restoration

You may remember the story of the prodigal son, who blew his inheritance on worldly living. Do you remember what happened next? Here is the account, beginning with the son's plan to return home:

"I will set out and go back to my father and say to him: Father, I have sinned against heaven and against you. I am no longer worthy to be called your son; make me like one of your hired men." So he got up and went to his father.

But while he was still a long way off, his father saw him and was filled with compassion for him; he ran to his son, threw his arms around him and kissed him.

The son said to him, "Father, I have sinned against heaven and against you. I am no longer worthy to be called your son."

But the father said to his servants, "Quick! Bring the best robe and put it on him. Put a ring on his finger and sandals on his feet. Bring the fattened calf and kill it. Let's have a feast and celebrate. For this son of mine was dead and is alive again; he was lost and is found." So they began to celebrate.

—Luke 15:18–24

Jesus Himself gave us this model of a truly repentant attitude. Notice many of the implications that Jesus included in the son's confession and the father's reception. First, the son acknowledges that his sin has hurt both God and people: "I have sinned against heaven and against you."

Next, he humbles himself—and he does something very important that we often fail to do with God: He not only acknowledges his desperation and depravity in verse 19, but he also recognizes that he *doesn't deserve* his father's forgiveness and reception. "I am no longer worthy to be called your son," he says. "Make me like one of your hired men."

Often we call out to God with the assumption that He owes it to us to answer and deliver what we ask for. But we don't deserve anything at all! If I deserve anything, it is damnation in hell. *Anything* better than hell is an undeserved bonus! This false notion that God owes us His grace and forgiveness and love and blessings is right at the heart of our ingratitude toward Him for these things.[4]

Finally, notice the joyful reception. The father was thrilled that his son had come back to him, and he halted everything to throw a party for him, with everyone in attendance. In the same way, our Father is waiting with open arms for us to run back to Him, and we cannot imagine the celebration that takes place in heaven when we do.

Psalm 51: Getting Back in the Battle

Psalm 51 is perhaps the most common passage of Scripture used as a model for repentance. We sing choruses based on it. The songs capture the emotion and brokenness David felt after his affair with Bathsheba, but the most popular one I know, Keith Green's "Create in Me a Clean Heart," leaves out a most important verse. Let's look at the first thirteen verses:

> *Have mercy upon me, O God, according to thy lovingkindness: according unto the multitude of thy tender mercies blot out my transgressions. Wash me thoroughly from mine iniquity, and cleanse me from*

my sin. For I acknowledge my transgressions: and my sin is ever before me. Against thee, thee only, have I sinned, and done this evil in thy sight: that thou mightest be justified when thou speakest, and be clear when thou judgest. Behold, I was shapen in iniquity; and in sin did my mother conceive me. Behold, thou desirest truth in the inward parts: and in the hidden part thou shalt make me to know wisdom.

Purge me with hyssop, and I shall be clean: wash me, and I shall be whiter than snow. Make me to hear joy and gladness; that the bones which thou hast broken may rejoice. Hide thy face from my sins, and blot out all mine iniquities. Create in me a clean heart, O God; and renew a right spirit within me. Cast me not away from thy presence; and take not thy holy spirit from me. Restore unto me the joy of thy salvation; and uphold me with thy free spirit. Then will I teach transgressors thy ways; and sinners shall be converted unto thee.

—KJV

David began in anguish over his sin, recognizing how awfully rotten he was. He acknowledged that he is truly guilty before God, and God's judgment of him is just. He pleaded with God several times to be washed of the sin, confident that God alone could make him clean and pure again. He wrote that not only did he need to be cleansed, but he needed the joy of his salvation restored to him as well.

David is not a happy guy here, and he doesn't have the energy to go on. This is where the Keith Green song ends (focused on verse 12), leaving out a most important part. But read verses 12 and 13 again. At the point where his joy is restored, he will be ready for ministry again; he's going to "teach transgressors [God's] ways and sinners will be converted unto [Him]." The reason so many of us guys feel worthless and apathetic toward ministry—we've lost our joy and we're devastated with guilt over sin. Why would we want to go and tell someone about Jesus when we feel so depressed and rotten about ourselves?

Take your sin to God and wait for Him to restore your joy, and you'll be amazed at your zeal and effectiveness for the Lord!

We know that we need to repent for our sins, so let's do it. We start by seeing our sin as God sees it, and God's grace as God sees it as well. Psalms 38–40, Luke 15, and Psalm 51 show us what a truly repentant heart looks like, and what a gracious, forgiving Father we have.

Today is not the last time we will need to repent, however. We will mess up again, and when we do, we must run back to the Lord with a heart full of grief for our sin, recognizing that sin for what it is, but then recognizing God's grace for all that it is and then press on in *victory!* We will see improvement, yes; if we take heed of the practical advice in these chapters, we will see great improvement and progress. But we will still stumble, and when we do we must repent. Brother, let us praise our great God for His sufficient and abundant grace!

Songs of Repentance

Singing can be a great way of communicating with the Lord. That's probably why so many of those closest to the Lord used song throughout the Bible. If you've sinned, try communicating your disdain for that sin and your desire for holiness and renewed fellowship with your sweet Savior through a song. The words to some of the most popular and powerful songs of repentance can be found on the Internet.

(More on the wise use of the Internet in chapter 8.) Three I highly commend are Keith Green's "Create in Me a Clean Heart," "Holiness," by Scott Underwood, and "Refiner's Fire" (also known as "Purify My Heart"), by Brian Doerksen.

REFLECTIONS

1. *Why are you running from sin? Do you seek to mortify all sins that bother God, or just the ones that bother you? Do you hate sin because of the consequences, including guilt and shame, or because God hates it and it grieves Him?*

2. *Which passage of Scripture in this chapter strikes you the most? Why?*

3. *When was the last time that you repented of your sins and turned back to God? What's holding you back from doing so today?*

Take some time today to pour your heart out to God, examining your attitude and approach to repentance, confessing your sins to Him, and then spend some time in thanksgiving and praise for all that He's saved you from.

❝ Most men have a hard time sustaining any sort of devotional life because it has no vital connection to recovering and protecting their strength; it feels about as important as flossing. But if you saw your life as a great battle and you *knew* you needed time with God for your very survival, you would do it.

JOHN ELDREDGE
Wild at Heart

How can a young man keep his way pure? **By living according to your word.** *. . . I have hidden your word in my heart that I might not sin against you.*

Psalm 119:9, 11 (emphasis added)

CHAPTER 5

How a Warrior Prepares

T H I N K of this war on sin as a real war. Being born again into God's family is like gaining citizenship to the country to which you want to belong. In a war, most nations are concerned with only protecting their own, so it's important to be part of that nation. Repenting is like clearing your criminal record and joining the army. We'll pretend that in this country you're a victim unless you're a soldier, so joining the army is imperative. Then, believing in God's promises is like believing that your nation is superior to the enemy nation and that you will have ultimate victory in the end—and that you have the capability of winning every battle along the way.

So now we're citizens of this great country, our criminal record has been wiped away, we've joined the army, and we believe we'll win the war. So what? We're certainly not ready to win any battles yet.

We must understand one thing about our enemy: He is cunning and crafty. He has many different weapons and knows how to use them at our weakest points. And the Evil One has been around a lot longer than we have. We can't just waltz into battle with a goofy grin on our face and expect to win. Pretend this war on sin is like the war against the evil forces in *The Lord of the Rings*. We're going up against the most skillful and ruthless Uruk-Hai there are. If we show up dressed like we're on our way to a tennis match, we'll get torn to pieces!

We're in a nasty war, and we have to train ourselves and become equipped with the right ammunition if we're going to win these battles against sexual temptation. The mere fact that you and I have lost so many battles, even as Christians, proves that something different must be done. Here are three ways to prepare for battle: (1) prayer, (2) Bible study and memorization, and (3) a battle plan.

Admit Your Dependence on Christ: Prayer

Nothing will contribute to your victory more than the help of the Lord Jesus Christ and the Holy Spirit in your life. You know that you are going to be tempted throughout the day, so pray before the day begins! Make prayer the very *first* thing you do in the morning, even before you have the opportunity to sin. Make prayer the *last* thing you do at night, so that your heart and mind are in the right place before you sleep and dream.

Listen to the Lord: Bible Study

Talking to God in prayer is important, but *listening* to God is just as important. Yes, God can talk to us through prayer as well, but His primary mode of communication to us is through His written Word, the Bible. Hey, everything significant that we've learned about overcoming temptation up to this point has come straight out of God's Word!

Think of Bible study as the training—and memorization as the weaponry—that the soldiers receive. If you think I'm crazy for comparing our struggle with sexual sin with a battle scenario, then consider this passage from Ephesians:

> *Finally, be strong in the Lord and in his mighty power. Put on the full armor of God so that you can take your stand against the devil's schemes. For our struggle is not against flesh and blood, but against the rulers, against the authorities, against the powers of this dark world and against the spiritual forces of evil in the heavenly realms. Therefore put on the full armor of God, so that when the day of evil comes, you may be able to stand your ground, and after you have done everything, to stand. Stand firm then, with the belt of truth buckled around your waist, with the breastplate of righteousness in place, and with your feet fitted with the readiness that comes from the gospel of peace. In addition to all this, take up the shield of faith, with which you can extinguish all the flaming arrows of the evil one. Take the helmet of salvation and the sword of the Spirit, which is the word of God. And pray in the Spirit on all occasions with all kinds of prayers and requests. With this in mind, be alert and* always keep on praying *for all the saints.*
>
> —Ephesians 6:10–18 (emphasis added)

If you haven't already, develop or find a plan to follow that will keep you accountable to daily Bible study. You might try getting a *One-Year Bible,* which will help you to read through the entire Bible in a year. If you've never read the entire Bible on your own, I suggest that you do it this year. Here is one brother's testimony (Daniel, age twenty) about the powerful effect that prayer and Bible study have in his personal battle for purity:

"I start each morning by stopping everything and getting alone with my Lord. I talk to Him and read His Word, and I ask Him every morning to renew my mind for that day. I ask for forgiveness and start the day righteous. This helps so much it is amazing. When I don't dedicate my mind to the Lord, that's when I find myself being attacked harder than normal."

Fighting the Lies of the Enemy

Many times the enemy can win battles because either we don't know or we don't believe what God has already promised in His Word. Psalm 119:105 says, "Your word is a lamp to my feet and a light for my path." Take away that light, and we'll stumble and fall. So many times I and countless other guys have fallen because we've accepted lies like, "You're overcome by temptation, so now you must indulge," "God is trying to ruin our fun and make our lives boring," "You've already sinned by looking at bad images, so it won't be any worse to masturbate to them," and of course, "You've sinned too much; God will no longer forgive you."

To counter these lies and live in the truth, we need to find, believe, and remember the promises God gives in the Bible that negate these lies. Please look up the following verses, and remember them along with the promises that they prove.

Promises That Can Defeat the Enemy

Promise 1:

> *Righteousness and fellowship with Jesus is better than sin.*
>
> —John 10:10

Promise 2:

> *We have not been tempted beyond what we can bear.*
>
> —1 Corinthians 10:13

Promise 3:

> *God will always provide a way out.*
>
> —1 Corinthians 10:13

Promise 4:

> *Jesus can help us when we are tempted.*
>
> —Hebrews 4:15–16

Promise 5:

> *If we resist the devil, he will flee from us.*
>
> —James 4:7

Promise 6:

> *If we draw near to God, he shall draw near to us.*
>
> —James 4:7–8

Promise 7:

> *We were not created for sin.*
>
> —Jeremiah 29:11

Promise 8:

I'm dead to that!

—Romans 6:2, 6–7, 11, 17–18

Promise 9:

God's grace is greater than all our sins.

—Ephesians 2:4–5, 8–9

Promise 10:

Jesus is coming soon to get us!

—Matthew 24:12–13, 42, 44

And in the Heat of Battle: Memorize Scripture

However important it is, merely reading and studying the Bible is not enough to become equipped to win battles against temptation, especially sexual temptation. We also have to *memorize Scripture.*

When we're tempted sexually, everything happens very fast. Decisions are made fast, either for good or for bad. Think of a time when you sinned with masturbation, pornography, or going too far with a girl. Just a few minutes ago everything was fine! *How did* this *happen?* we find ourselves asking. We won't always have a Bible with us to look up verses we've studied about purity and holiness, and even if we did, we probably wouldn't go to all the trouble of looking them up in the first place. We've actually got to *write these things on our hearts and minds.* "Anyone serious about purity must be able to recall Scripture *instantaneously;* there sometimes isn't time to talk to Christian brothers or look up a Bible passage," explains Robert Daniels, a minister and former addict to pornography.[1] We can only do this if we memorize Scripture.

Throughout history, God's people have been memorizing Scripture. The Israelites did during the time of the kingdom and beyond, and Christians did it in the early church and beyond. Our best example is in our commander and general in this war, Jesus Christ. Remember Promise 4 above? Jesus was tempted just as we are, so we can run to Him for help when we are tempted. And how did Jesus overcome temptation? *Scripture memory!* Jesus knew the Word of His Father, and He used it. In all three times that Satan tempted Jesus in the desert, Jesus quoted Scripture. You can read it in Luke 4. Jesus had studied the Bible and knew it so well that even when Satan quoted a verse to Him, Jesus knew that Satan had taken the verse out of context and He knew another passage that would set the devil straight (verses 10–12).

When I'm afraid of something, I quote Psalm 23 from memory. When I am tempted to sin sexually, I cry out to God and begin to quote Scripture that I have memorized. Oh, it is such a powerful tool! A thought comes into my head that is unwholesome, and I just say, "I take every thought captive and make it obedient to Christ! I take every thought captive and make it obedient to Christ!" (see 2 Corinthians 10:5) or one of a number of similar Scriptures,[2] and after a couple of times that thought is history. *I resisted the devil, and he fled from me!*

Oh, how I praise God for His Word! It truly *is* sharper than any two-edged sword! "For the word of God is living and active. Sharper than any double-edged sword, it penetrates even to dividing soul and spirit, joints and marrow; it judges the thoughts and attitudes of the heart" (Hebrews 4:12). Memorizing Scripture is perhaps the most important thing we can do in preparation for the battles to come.

Study It, Memorize It, and *Live* It!

One more thing about Bible study and memorization. Recall the words of Psalm 119:9: "How can a young man keep his way pure? By *living* according to your word" (italics added). Reading the Bible is certainly not enough, and even memorizing the Bible is still not enough; *we have to live what we learn!* That's the point of James when he discusses hypocrisy: "Do not merely listen to the word, and so deceive yourselves. Do what it says. . . . The man who looks intently into the perfect law that gives freedom, and continues to do this, not forgetting what he has heard, but doing it—he will be blessed in what he does" (James 1:22, 25).

Draw Up a Battle Plan

There is one more thing we need to do before the battle begins: develop a battle plan. Without such a plan, if we're caught in the midst of temptation and haven't thought about a decision ahead of time, we're probably going to follow our carnal desire. For this reason, we have to anticipate situations before they occur—and determine how we're going to respond. This applies to lust, masturbation, pornography, premarital sex, and every other sexual sin that you can think of. I'll expound on this more in the next several chapters. But right now, start drafting your battle plan!

This plan should include all the practical steps you are going to take to stay pure and run from temptation, beginning with prayer, repentance, Bible study, and Bible memorization. Include *what* Scripture passages you plan to memorize, and *when* you will have them memorized by. Some key passages to start with are:

- ## Psalm 119:9, 11, 105
- ## 2 Timothy 2:22

- **1 Corinthians 10:12–13**
- **Job 31:1**
- **Ephesians 6:10–18**

Don't get caught off guard. Prepare yourself. If you have things in your life that are just making your battle more difficult, get rid of them. "Pray in the Spirit on all occasions with all kinds of prayers and requests" (Ephesians 6:18), hold fast to the promises of God, and hide His Word in your heart and mind so it automatically comes up in the heat of battle. Then gear up, because the enemy is ready and war is upon us.

REFLECTIONS

1. *Sit down and prayerfully develop a battle plan. Include how you'll get rid of or avoid those things that will make your struggle more difficult, and which things you need to integrate into your life to help you prepare for battle. A card for developing a battle plan, along with key Scripture verses, is located inside the back cover of this book.*

2. *Share this list with a trusted friend or mentor, and ask him to hold you to this plan.*

>> If there is an Enemy of Souls (and I have not the slightest doubt that there is), one thing he cannot abide is the desire for purity. Hence a man or woman's passions become his battleground. The Lover of Souls does not prevent this. I was perplexed because it seemed to me He should prevent it, but He doesn't. He wants us to learn to use our weapons.

ELISABETH ELLIOT
Passion and Purity

Run from anything that stimulates youthful lust. . . . Flee the evil desires of youth. . . . Flee also from youthful lusts. . . .

2 Timothy 2:22: NLT, NIV, and KJV, respectively

CHAPTER 6

In the Battle

WE'VE joined the army, we've gone to training (which we'll have to continually keep going back to throughout the entire war), and we have our super-sharp, double-edged sword and armor. We're ready to fight! Bring on the enemy!

Well, that should never be our attitude with sexual sin, since the best thing we're going to do is to *run* anyway! We do not welcome the temptation of any sin, especially sexual sin.

If we follow carefully all that we've learned to this point, the Lord Jesus will be drawing us close to Him and renewing our minds so that we will be like Him. We also need practical, sound advice about what we should do when each flaming arrow comes at us: temptations to lust, masturbate, view pornography, fondle a girl, have sex, and every other sexual temptation that we will face. Those listed here are the ones that I will specifically address in the upcoming chapters.

In the next four chapters, we're going to go to work. We're gonna stretch ourselves way out of our comfort zones. But when we're all done, we'll be so glad we did. We're going to consider some rock-solid principles that apply to all sexual sins, and then we're going to nail the four biggies one by one: lust, pornography, masturbation, and improper sexual relationships. God's Word is full of wisdom, so we will find a lot of ammo there. But that's only the beginning: I've talked to a whole lot of guys just like you and me, and they have shared many of the awesome things that God has done in their lives to drive a silver stake right into the heart of their greatest struggles. So without further ado, let's do this.

Prayer, Scripture Recital, and Dependency on Christ

The day has begun and we're all prayed-up and ready to go. We've spent time in Bible study and we're armed with those powerful and effective verses that will destroy any argument the enemy has for us to sin. We're ready to go! But while we go, we need to remember prayer, Scripture, and dependency on Christ most of all. When faced with a temptation, first of all pray. Pray honestly to the Lord, and pray in the name of Jesus Christ. Brother, the enemy does *not like* that name!

All the while you're doing this, keep your eyes focused on Jesus Christ, because without Him we're toast. So tell Him this throughout the day: "Lord, I cannot do this without You. But with You, I know that I can do anything! For 'I can do all things through Christ who strengthens me.'" And while you pray, recite the Scripture that you've memorized.

General Solutions

In each one of the situations we will consider, there are three general solutions. Each is universal.

First, *run!* If you're tempted by the Internet, *run.* If things are getting too hot on your date, *run.* (Well, take her home first if you can. Then run.) If you know you're going to masturbate . . . yes, *run.* If you're lusting after a billboard or girl walking by . . . *run.* How you do this will be different in each situation, but it's all going to come down to fleeing from the thing that is causing your youthful lust.

Second, with each one of these temptations you need to *develop a solid battle plan.* I know which temptations are the worst for me, and I've carefully crafted a plan to avoid each temptation and to get rid of it when it comes. Develop this battle plan with your accountability partner or your mentor—which we'll talk about further along in the book.

When the temptation comes, no matter what it is, scream, "I'm Dead to That!" in the face of the temptation (Romans 6:14). This admonition is advocated strongly by pastor and author James MacDonald. (Don't actually scream that at your girlfriend, however; you'll scare her. Scaring girls—bad! Be gentle.) Remember all of the promises of God, especially this one and the two from 1 Corinthians 10:13— any temptation is common to others too, and God will provide a way to escape.

Time for a Tourniquet

Here's the final general solution to remember before we start "going rounds" with each individual sin category: Sometimes you need to *apply a tourniquet.* Here's a medical analogy as we prepare for spiritual battle. In a battle, many people are wounded. I've learned about first aid both as a lifeguard and in the military. If you are cut or your skin is broken open in some way, you want to apply pressure to the wound in order to stop the bleeding. You have to be careful of infection, but the first priority is to stop the bleeding. You want to apply a steady amount of pressure, but not too much. If you apply too much pressure, especially at the joint, you risk cutting off all blood flow to that part of the body. If that happens, the part may have to be amputated. That's why you want to use a bandage with *some* pressure, so that the blood can still flow and keep that body part alive.

Sometimes, however, the injury is so bad and the wound so severe that the blood flow needs to be cut off to that part of the body. The person is bleeding so badly that if the bleeding is not stopped, *he or she will die.* The injured is in desperate shape. This is when it's time to apply a tourniquet. A tourniquet is something —typically a strap of rubber or piece of fabric—that is wrapped so tightly around a part of the body that it stops all blood flow to anything beyond the tourniquet.

Tourniquets are rarely applied, because medics know that if they use them the injured person will probably lose whatever is beyond the tourniquet—usually a limb. These were used more in World War II and before, when there weren't more modern ways to save the limb like there are today. That is why so many wounded WWII veterans are without an arm or a leg. But even though their lives have become very inconvenient without that limb, those veterans are alive today and probably are very grateful for the tourniquet's role in keeping them alive.

This same principle needs to be applied to our daily

lives and our struggle with sexual sin. There are times when we can apply a bandage to the situation: changing the relationship, getting an Internet filter, or some other thing that will allow us to keep that privilege or "limb." But there are other times when we have to be honest with ourselves and apply the tourniquet. This might mean ending the relationship or getting rid of the computer or television. It's going to hurt and inconvenience us, but we have to because we'll die without it! We probably won't physically die (unless we get a lethal STD or get ourselves shot by some angry girl's boyfriend, dad, or brother) and we will still be saved, but the sin will ruin our life if we don't take drastic action. This is not going to be any fun, but we'll be much better off in the long run if we do it.

I didn't come up with this tourniquet idea myself; Jesus did. Check this out: "If your right eye causes you to sin, gouge it out and throw it away. It is better for you to lose one part of your body than for your whole body to be thrown into hell. And if your right hand causes you to sin, cut it off and throw it away. It is better for you to lose one part of your body than for your whole body to go into hell" (Matthew 5:29–30).

Pray about this; start asking the Lord if there is some area of your life where you need to apply a tourniquet. If there is, be bold enough to do it. Ask an accountability partner or mentor to help you. (But don't take this analogy too far. The tourniquet principle does not work for every situation.)

OK, we've looked at some powerful pieces of ammunition and how they apply to our battle for purity. We've seen how we need to pray, recite Scripture, and depend on Christ with each temptation. We also must run from each temptation that comes our way, and adjust or add to our plan as we face new challenges. Finally, our resolve that we're dead to sin must be so strong that we're willing to apply a tourniquet if nothing else is working. Now let's start hitting these sins one by one and learning some practical steps to get them under control.

REFLECTIONS

1. *Which of the four areas (lust, pornography, masturbation, and relationships) is your greatest struggle? In which other area do you struggle?*

2. *Before we look at the next four chapters, do you already know an area where you need to apply a tourniquet?*

**   ** No thought should be allowed to have its own way . . . When Christ is in control of our lives, the Holy Spirit is in power. When we let the old man—the sinful nature—be in control, then the Spirit is quenched. The solution is to bring every thought captive; and if we find we have sinned, confess it, and ask Christ to again take control. That's the essence of living by the power of the Holy Spirit.

PATRICK MORLEY
The Man in the Mirror

*We demolish arguments and every pretension that sets itself up against the knowledge of God, and **we take every thought captive to make it obedient to Christ.***

2 Corinthians 10:5 (emphasis added)

CHAPTER 7

Lust: Where the Battle Starts

L U S T . Our oldest enemy. The most frequent of all our sexual sins, and quite possibly of all our sins in general. We can lust after many things, such as power, money, and status (1 John 2:16), but this chapter deals specifically with physical lust.

Before we have sex or do any sexual act outside of marriage, we lust. When we sin by looking at pornography, we lust. When we masturbate, we lust. Jesus said lust is as bad as adultery, and many times we consider adultery the worst of all these sins. So it's a pretty bad problem that we need to deal with. And there's no tourniquet for this baby either, because even gouging out our eyes wouldn't cure lust, as we can still lust with just our minds.

D. L. Moody illustrated how tolerating just a little lust can quickly lead to other things that are more destructive:

> When I was speaking to five thousand children in Glasgow some years ago, I took a spool of thread and said to one of the largest boys: "Do you believe I can bind you with that thread?"
> He laughed at the idea. I wound the thread around him a few times, and he broke it with a single jerk. Then I wound the thread around and around, and by and by I said: "Now get free if you can."
> He couldn't move head or foot. If you are slave to some vile habit, you must either slay that habit or it will slay you.[1]

Lust certainly is a tricky little devil. I'm not writing as one who has completely gotten rid of all lust from his life. I can think of a time when I lusted today, in fact. I repented of that sin, and I will make a point of avoiding that temptation the next time I'm in that same situation. But there will always be more and more opportunities to lust, and it will only get worse as society lowers its standards for what women should wear and what media can expose us to.

However, there is hope! Although no Christian men are totally free from lustful thoughts, I've talked with many guys who have made an incredible amount of progress in their lives over this sin. And, thank God, so have I. I do remember a time when my mind was clouded with lustful thoughts practically all day long; now an indulged sexual thought is the exception that stands out, and I usually repent of it quickly and move on.

There are many clear steps that we can take to run from lust and gain sexual purity, even in our minds. Remember, God said that He wasn't going to give us more temptation than we could handle and that He would always provide a way out (1 Corinthians 10:13), and that applies even to the temptation to lust. Here are some practical ways to run away from a lustful situation.

How to Escape Lustful Situations:

1. Recite Scripture

As always, pray first. While you're praying, call to your mind some of those Scriptures that you've memorized. Have them ready and shoot them like darts at your tempting thought, while at the same time darting your eyes or mind away from that temptation. Like Job (31:1), you should be able to tell yourself, *I've made a covenant with my eyes not to look lustfully at a girl! I've made a covenant with my eyes not to look lustfully at a girl!* Say this over and over again. Say it out loud if you can!

Find some catchy phrases that will stick in your mind and that will be effective in your life when you use them. When I was a lifeguard at an amusement park, there was temptation to lust literally *everywhere I turned!* I had never seen so many scantily clad women in all my life, and I was around them all day long! This was torture on my hormones. It was either indulge myself all day long, or else find out some ways to run. And while I did look lustfully at the women many times, I spent the majority of the time *running* from lust. Here's a mind trick I came up with: Every time my eyes would get drawn to a girl's body, I would scream in my mind, *Not mine, don't look!* Over and over again in my mind I said, *Not mine, don't look!* I must have said that one little phrase more than 10,000 times to myself over the course of the summer. And it worked, too! I was in prayer, praying for my purity, and praying for these people as well.

Reciting Scripture or scriptural principles is a key way to combat lust.

2. Look at Women from the Chin Up

When I was in high school I noticed these guys who always walked around with their heads hung low, and they never looked anyone in the eye. I always felt bad for these guys, because I thought that they were depressed or something. But soon enough I found out: They weren't depressed, they were just staring at all the girls' butts as they walked down the hallway! OK, they might have *also* been depressed, but they were definitely on butt-watch patrol.

In order to stop lusting after women as objects, we need to see them as human beings, and in order to see them as human beings we need to *see* them as such; we need to look them in the eye. This is a rule that I've had for myself for quite a while: Anything below the chin is *off-limits!*

This doesn't mean that we should not look at girls at all. The issue is *where* and *how* we look at girls. It is OK to admire and even be attracted to parts of a girl's face, which often give clues to her heart. It's a wonderful thing to have an attractive girl smile at you, and to smile back at her, and there's nothing wrong with that. In your heart you know the difference between looking at a girl as a person and a friend, and looking at a girl as an object. Girls certainly know the difference as well.

Lust is more than sexual thoughts—it's longing for or coveting a girl who is not ours. The problem is not just belittling the girl with our lust. For some, lust is so closely tied to worship—we're longing for something to worship and our eyes fix on something tangible, something that we can see and admire and say, *Hey, I can worship this.* We need to recognize that she's not the goddess we make her out to be, nor is she an object. She is a person.

A friend of mine pointed something out to me the other day that really put this in perspective. He explained that when he looks at other guys, he is trying to understand them; he is looking at their eyes to learn what is in their heart. Seeing is a huge part of communication between guys. We need to look at girls with the same dignity that we look at guys with. Not with a selfish, covetous gaze that oozes shallowness and either makes her uncomfortable or causes her to stumble, but with a sincere, respectful look that builds her up as a human being and a child of God. There's much more to it than just keeping our eyes off her body, but looking at women from the chin up is a great start.

3. Pray *for* Her!

Going along with this whole "View her as a person and not an object" idea, try *praying for the girl* when you see her. Sure, at first your prayers might be along the lines of, "Lord, please bless this woman with a bigger shirt or a job as a nun," but eventually you will start to earnestly pray for the daughter of God that you're passing or that you're talking to. It's a great strategy and it works. Try it today. She is a person, just like your sister or a friend's sister. Speaking of which . . .

4. Picture Her as Your Sister

There are four women in this world whom I love more than anyone else. They are my wonderful mother and my three amazing sisters, Ellen, Susan, and Jane. I would do anything for any one of them, and I get absolutely ticked when I hear that anyone has done anything to hurt them or offend them. I also have no problem whatsoever under-standing that each one of *them* is a precious and beloved daughter of the Most High God, and I demand that I and everyone else treat them as nothing less than that. I become much more leery of the world when I consider my sisters.

One of my best friends believes the "sister view" is the way to go. "Whenever you see a woman whom you're attracted to, begin thinking of her as a sister, even praying for her as a sister. If it's necessary, imagine that person being your actual sister—that, for most guys, cools off the lust because it suggests something that most people would be absolutely disgusted with."

Darren, who is twenty-one, then adds, "Keeping with this sister theme—imagine what you would do to another guy who even thought about your sister the way you're thinking of this girl. Most guys are fiercely protective of their sister's safety—the idea of a guy touching her wrong is stronger than most any other instinct I can think of. I threaten my sister's many 'pursuers' with my 32-inch, 27-ounce Easton metal baseball bat that consistent years of baseball, softball, and batting cages have enabled me to swing at terrifying velocities. I have to threaten myself too."

We become a little more honest about the way things are when our sisters and mothers are involved. But wait, something doesn't add up here: If we are children of God and these girls are also children of God, then that must mean that we're both . . . siblings! These girls *are* our sisters!

So why doesn't *that* relationship change things? Oh, because we might marry one of them and then we'll be allowed to have sex with her? But the problem is that we will *at best* marry *just one* of these people we call girls, and all the rest of them will never be our wife! Besides, absolutely none of them is our wife right now, so there is *no one* that we may have sexual thoughts about.

5. Occupy Your Mind

I know that occupying your mind is a tough task, but there are so many other thoughts to think! Take up a sport, learn to fix cars, become a marine, write a book, go to college, go to high school: do something productive with your brain today! Can you imagine the potential we guys would have if we channeled all the mental energy we invest in thinking about women into something productive? We'd be colonizing Mars and taking vacations to Jupiter by now!

I pray that these strategies will have a significant impact in your life as you battle these temptations. Before we conclude our discussion on lust, we need to address a couple of other issues.

Look Out for Your Brother

This thing is not just all about you, and it's not about me. It is not enough to look out only for ourselves, and abstain from something only if it causes us to stumble or sin personally. *We are commanded to look out for our brothers and sisters in Christ as much as we look out for ourselves.* Consider these words from Paul: "Accept him whose faith is weak, without passing judgment on disputable matters. . . . Therefore, let us stop passing judgment on one another. Instead, *make up your mind not to put any stumbling block or obstacle in your brother's way*" (Romans 14:1, 13; emphasis added).

We need to make up our minds that we're not going to do anything, say anything, or have anything available that will cause our friends to stumble into sexual sin, including lust. I had an experience some time ago where I had to go the extra mile to keep from causing my brothers to sin because of something I had in my room. During my freshman year in college, some weightlifting magazines were lying around my room that had pictures of nearly naked women. Many people would say that there's nothing wrong with this, because we honestly had them to learn about nutrition and weightlifting. But when some guys came into my room and looked through the magazines, they lusted and sinned. I couldn't allow that to happen again, so I got rid of the magazines the next day, and I've been careful ever since not to have anything that will cause anyone else to stumble, even if it doesn't bother me personally.

Don't take lightly the warning from Jesus when He said, "Things that cause people to sin are bound to come, but woe to that person through whom they come. It would be better for him to be thrown into the sea with a millstone tied around his neck than for him to cause one of these little ones to sin. So watch yourselves" (Luke 17:1–3). When it comes to sexual temptation, we must look out for our brother. Whether it's magazines, posters, crude jokes, or even pictures of our female friends, we need to be careful not to distract other Christian guys or cause them to stumble. Look out for your brother.

Don't Even Stick Your Toe in the Door

As I mentioned earlier, we will never mosey into sexual purity. As a roommate of mine once said, "Don't tolerate just a little sin, because sin doesn't tolerate just a little of you." Sexual sin is one of the most vicious, deliberate, and devastating kinds of sin I have ever seen. I have seen friends of *all* ages almost crushed under its powerful arm of destruction, and it's not pretty. People can have great and glorious plans for their future, and then suddenly they are crushed by some sexual mistake. They get their girlfriend pregnant. They contract a sexually transmitted disease. Infidelity destroys their marriage. Their world is turned upside down because of a heated night of passion.

Be Like Joseph (Not Me . . . the One in the Bible!)

The only chance we have at victory is to not even give sexual sin a chance. Consider Joseph in the book of Genesis. When Potiphar's wife was coming on to him, he didn't stick around to give her some godly counsel and try to get to the root of her problem; he *ran* out the door! She grabbed at his clothes and he simply fled. If something is causing you to sin, *get rid of it*.

I imagine that King David could have taken a lesson from his forefather Joseph. One day David was on the roof and saw Bathsheba taking a bath. His lust burned for her so fiercely that he commanded her to come to his palace and had sex with her, a married woman. Then he murdered and lied to cover up his actions. Imagine: adultery, murder, and the big lie, all because of wanting to satisfy a lust.

I wonder how many times he recalled that day and thought to himself, *Why didn't you just get off the stinking roof? Note to self for the future: stay off roof. Better yet, maybe I should just move!*

God has provided us two very vivid examples for us to observe, so that we can make the right decision. Take the *right* action. Run away! Get off the roof! Do whatever it takes!

Do you need to burn some calendars or magazines? Do it! Do you need to replace the picture of that sexy lady on your computer? How about substituting a photo of a nice kitten? OK, you can go with a monster truck—but only if there's not a lady in a string bikini next to it! Whatever the temptation is in your life, get rid of it. Whatever you need to do to keep from presenting your brother with a stumbling block, please do it! The rest of your life will thank you for it.

Winning Strategies

Lust is the genesis of our war with sexual temptation. If we want to have any chance of not becoming a casualty in this war, it has to start here. We have to fight to win our minds back with strategies like prayer, reciting Scripture, looking at women from the chin up, praying for women we think about, and occupying our minds. While we do, we must not forget to look out for our brother, and to be like Joseph by not even sticking our toe in the door of sin.

If we get serious about fighting back in the battle for our minds, then fighting the other battles will become much easier.

REFLECTIONS

1. *What strategies have you read here that you could add to your battle plan?*

2. *What other strategies can you think of that will help you when you are most tempted to lust?*

> I know that pornography damages and eventually destroys individuals, marriages, and families. But I also know that you don't have to be crushed by giving in to lust, and you don't have to pass it on to your sons. The battle can be won, but we must be prepared . . . and be willing to fight!
>
> *Triumph Over Temptation: For the Single Man*[1]

When tempted, no one should say, "God is tempting me." For God cannot be tempted by evil, nor does he tempt anyone; but each one is tempted when, by his own evil desire, he is dragged away and enticed. Then, after desire has conceived, it gives birth to sin; and sin, when it is full-grown, gives birth to death.

James 1:13–15

CHAPTER 8

Pornography: You Can Break Free

MY FRIEND Dan told me the story of how a curiosity sparked by steamy scenes in TV situation comedies fell into a regular diet of pornography:

"I started going online and searching for pictures of the actresses I would see on TV. The pictures I saw would just get me hooked for more and more images. I knew what time of the week that I would have the house to myself, and those were the times when I would have my fun on the Internet. Each night after looking at the pictures, I would feel so empty and so pathetic. It was a very lonely feeling."

With the help of prayer and a trusted spiritual leader, Dan was able to wean himself off of the unwholesome pictures and overcome this struggle. He recalled a few lessons that he learned:

"Through my experience with pornography, I realized a few things. First, once I got a taste of it, I was like a glutton at an all-you-can-eat restaurant. I just wanted more of it. I could not get enough. Second, my lust for women was not just contained to the TV and pictures. From those things, it spread to real people in everyday life—lusting after class-mates and other girls. My eyes would wander, and I liked what I saw. Though I have been free from the Internet stuff for years now, the casual glances are the toughest things to break. I see now that my choice of TV shows led to years of trouble down the road."

An Absolute Danger

Pornography is absolutely dangerous. It can ruin your life, and it has ruined many lives already. Nothing in my life has ever made me feel filthier than when I've viewed pornography, and no other sin has been more destructive in my life. It's by the grace of God that I'm where I am today: still a student at Cedarville University, still an Air Force officer candidate, still a child of God.

Except for the child of God part, pornography could have ruined all of that, including my reputation and my relationship with everyone I love. I praise God that I'm where I am today, and I'll praise Him as long as I live for having mercy on me and giving me victory over this sin.

You'd better believe that it's God who deserves all of the glory for all of this, because without Him I'm simply a miserable wretch.

I'm not the only Christian guy who has fallen into pornography. In fact, *the majority* of Christian guys that I interviewed admitted that pornography is or has been a major struggle for them. I don't tell you this to make you think it's OK; I tell it to you so that you can gain hope from the fact that you are not alone, and that many of us are having *victory* over this sin. We have to take this sin seriously, because it can wreck our lives and make us useless to God.

Check out a few testimonies from some good friends of mine who want desperately to warn others about how sinning even a little bit can have a devastating avalanche effect on your life.

Pornography and lust affected every other area of my life. It affected my relationship with God. I lost the peace and love in my heart for His Word. It affected my love for life. I grew cynical and skeptical of God's provision. It affected my relationships with men and women tenfold. As I sank deeper in the crevices of my desire, I lost touch with many of my closest friends around me. I grew selfish in my time with people. I even found it difficult to give them my full attention without worrying about my shame and guilt.

John, 23

I wish I would have known just how addicting pornography really is. Stay away! There is nothing more destructive than being naïve to the destruction that is headed their way if they just dabble in it.

Ryan, 22

Don't touch [pornography] at ALL! I stumbled onto some inappropriate magazines in my stepbrother's room back home just before I began high school and every year after that I was entrenched in sin and lust and gratification. It only takes one look that goes too long, and then comes a descending spiral that is impossible to pull yourself out of. Your body will demand more and more until you crave unspeakable things!

Steve, 20

Why does pornography ensnare so many guys? Because it's the quickest and easiest way to satisfy our desires—for sex, for female companionship. John Eldredge explains this in *Wild at Heart:*

> Most men want the maiden without any sort of cost to themselves. They want all the joys of the beauty without any of the woes of the battle. This is the sinister nature of pornography—enjoying the woman at her expense. Pornography is what happens when a man insists on being energized by a woman; he *uses* her to get a feeling that he is a man. It is a false strength, as I've said, because it depends on an outside source rather than emanating from deep within his center. And it is the paragon of selfishness. He offers nothing and takes everything.[2]

Beginning with Confession

How do we get out from under this terrible struggle? It starts with confession. Admitting that I've struggled with pornography has been the hardest thing about writing this book. My mom knows this now! My sisters know. And any girl who wants to can know as well.

To any sister in Christ who reads this and feels betrayed or angry I say this:

> *I'm sorry. You have a right to be angry. I have sinned against God and against you. But know this: I have repented of my sin and I am living in victory today! The Lord Jesus is so graciously renewing my mind. And I hate pornography and what it has done to women, and I've made every effort and will continue to make every effort necessary to ensure that it plays no part in my life. Please forgive me, dear sister, and believe that the Joe you get is not the Joe that once was,*

*by the grace and the mighty work of Christ Jesus our Savior.
Thank you.*

Have you told another Christian who loves you that you've struggled with pornography? If not, please do that today. Pray about who it should be. If you can trust your parents, tell them. Maybe it can be your pastor, or another man in your church whom you trust. But tell someone; don't fight this alone. Accountability is the first giant step toward victory.

One Late, Lonely Night . . .

Before I describe the things that God used in my life to gain victory over pornography, let me tell you the story of my struggle. I rarely struggled with pornography in junior high and high school. Maybe it was because I was living at home, and it would be too hard to look at those things and face my mom, my dad, and my sisters. Maybe it was because I was a Christian at a secular high school, and people were watching me to see how I would respond when they brought a magazine to the locker room. I don't know for sure, but the struggle started when I got to college.

For the first time I had Internet access right in my room, anytime I wanted. The Internet filters my school had in place helped me to avoid looking at pornography for the first two quarters of my freshman year. But when spring quarter rolled around, the filters couldn't keep me from stumbling any longer. I was completely burned out from all of the all-nighters I'd pulled and all of the activity I was involved in. Very late one night, something popped up on my computer, and I clicked onto it because I was just too tired to resist. What I clicked onto sparked an interest, and I clicked a few more times in order to see more. Those filters didn't detect those offensive sites. I looked quickly; then in a flash, I turned off the computer.

The whole encounter lasted less than a minute. I told someone the very next day, but I didn't do anything more about it because I thought that I was over it. I knew I could turn off my Internet access, but I didn't think I would need to. I was wrong. I gave in two more times that year, never for more than a few minutes at a time, until I finally had the Internet shut off.

The next year I came back all ready to do battle with sin. This was right after I wrote the journal entry in chapter 2, and I was excited because it had been months since I had even masturbated. I felt I would be fine to turn the Internet back on, and I was . . . for a while. I managed to go all of fall semester of my sophomore year without stumbling on the Internet, but the next semester I found myself right back where I was a year earlier.

I tried "bandages" for a while: making rules about when and how I would use the Internet, and I had plenty of accountability, but eventually this was not enough. It was time to apply the tourniquet, because I was bleeding so badly and it wasn't going to stop. So I had my Internet access shut off and I made the firm decision that I would leave it off until the day I graduated years later. I took this commitment home; I have chosen not to allow myself any Internet access at my house. If I really need to use the Internet, then the library is just five minutes away. It's a little bit inconvenient, but it's more than worth it!

I've kept the Internet off since that day, and I haven't struggled with it one time at school or at home since then. Praise God! Oh, brother, if being crippled by the sin of pornography is one of the worst feelings in the world, then being free from its clutches and walking in purity is one of the very best feelings in the world.

Winning Strategies

Whatever your story is, here are some strategies that I and others have learned to combat pornography.

1. Confession

As noted earlier, begin with confession. Your confession should be first to God, and then to someone you trust. This is covered in detail in chapter 11.

2. Apply the tourniquet

If you're struggling with pornography, then you probably need to do *something* drastic about it, because the trend is usually that guys only get sucked in further and further if they don't. Although applying the tourniquet is the last resort for gaining victory with a girl, it belongs next here. I don't know exactly what this will mean specifically for you, but ask the Lord and be willing to do whatever He tells you.

Here are a few clues as to how a tourniquet may be applied when it comes to staunching the bleeding from pornography. It may mean *getting rid of the cable or satellite dish completely.* Ouch. No more ESPN. But it's worth it! It may mean *cutting off all Internet access or getting rid of the computer.* Ouch. No more eBay. But it's worth it! If your struggle is with buying magazines or videos, then it may mean *not walking around with any more cash or credit cards,* or *avoiding all stores that sell anything pornographic.* I hope you can do the second of those two, because the first would be a real bummer. But the question is this: Would you be willing to do either? Bigger question: How much is this worth to you? How much do you hate this sin? How much do you love those who look up to you, and those who will someday look up to you (like your wife and kids)? God bless you as you consider what it is you need to do with this.

3. Use Internet filters

Blocking filters have value—but I must add that their value is limited. There are numerous ways to get around them, and adding them tightens the tourniquet only halfway, as filters won't catch all the garbage (for example, at my college they failed to block everything), and guys can often justify loosening the filters when they disallow legitimate sites that have offending words only occasionally. The conclusion I've come to about Internet filters is that they're most effective when one is not trying to look at pornography. But for guys like me, who have a weakness in this area, we need something more deliberate to help us avoid this temptation. There is a tool that works even better, that you can use in addition to filters. That tool is the fourth strategy for combating pornography.

4. Become accountable to someone by using computer software to monitor your Internet usage

If you choose to keep the Internet on your computer and have added Internet filters, stuff still can get through. Here is where accountability to another guy can be a big help. Install on your computer a program to monitor every single Web site you visit. The program I recommend will send an e-mail to an accountability partner or partners of your choice with every single URL you visited, no matter how short or long you were there. You cannot turn it off once it's on, and uninstalling it requires a code that you have to call *the vendor* to get—so you won't get out of it in a frenzied, lustful moment.

Let me introduce you to "Covenant Eyes." This is a wonderful tool to use, and one that I will use again if I ever allow myself to have any sort of Internet access after I graduate from college. I learned about it from Promise Keepers. I downloaded the program and used it at home for a while, and it worked just great. The program lets your accountability partner(s) view a list of every Web site you visited that week. As noted, you can have the program uninstalled by contacting Covenant Eyes, but doing so will generate an e-mail to your accountability partners, so you'll have to explain why you turned it off anyway.[3]

There are plenty of other strategies to combat pornography. Some of these include keeping your door open, facing the computer toward the door, or giving someone else the account password for the computer. I've even heard of a guy whose wife was the only one who knew the password to get on the computer, so she knew whenever he was on the Internet. I very well might try that after I marry, if my wife and I decide we need Internet access. Internet filters can be a good idea if they are helpful to you, but Covenant Eyes is even better because you can't easily get rid of the monitoring system. Consider carefully what you need to do to kill this devastating habit at the core. I've applied the tourniquet while I'm still in school, and I'm going to continue to make wise choices about television/cable and

Internet access in the future, recognizing the temptation and taking steps to run from it.

We have a choice. We can pursue the dreams and plans that God has laid on our hearts, or we can stay complacent, lethargic, defeated, and discredited by our struggle with pornography. We can't do both. Be concerned by your potential to fail, take heart because of your potential for victory, and go to war. Don't live one more day ruining your mind and your potential for the Lord.

REFLECTIONS

1. *Have you ever struggled with pornography of any kind, whether TV, magazines, movies, Internet, or anything else? When are you most vulnerable?*

2. *What steps will you take to break or prevent the habit of pornography in your life?*

❝ Bringing yourself to orgasm while thinking about anyone to whom you are not married is, according to Jesus, adultery. . . . Thinking about some sexual scenario and achieving an orgasm to those thoughts conditions you to what sex could be like. This is very dangerous in that it sets up unrealistic expectations for what sex with your wife—or future wife—should be like.

DR. MARK LAASER
"Man and Sex: Moving Beyond Selfishness"

Therefore, I urge you, brothers, in view of God's mercy, to offer your bodies as living sacrifices, holy and pleasing to God—this is your spiritual act of worship. Do not conform any longer to the pattern of this world, but be transformed by the renewing of your mind. Then you will be able to test and approve what God's will is—his good, pleasing and perfect will.

Romans 12:1–2

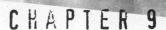

CHAPTER 9

Masturbation: Unmasking the Lie

A D A M , age twenty-one, describes the temptations most guys face in a sex-saturated society—the temptations to put their minds and eyes on girls instead of God.

"I wake up first thing in the morning with one thing on my mind: living for the Lord with all my heart, soul, and mind. I'm embracing the victory and ready to live out my faith at school and at work. I dig into Psalms and thank God that my help comes from the Maker (Psalm 121).

"I work at a local pool; it's the middle of the summer. I keep my eyes peeled to the ground, hoping to escape any ounce of temptation that could possibly come my way—then I look up.

"With one look at that girl comes one single thought. I

ignore it and continue with my job. Six p.m. comes and I drive home in my car. The worship music I usually have cranked becomes almost boring, so I switch to the Top 40 station. The songs on the way home have crazy sweet beats and the bass in my car is vibrating my trunk. The problem is, every song is loaded with sexual fantasies that cloud my vision.

"God is still on my mind and I plan out my evening so I can spend time with Him. I am tired, though, and I sit in front of the TV to rest. One hour . . . two hours . . . three hours have passed and I'm relaxed—but so is my mind. My heart that I was so willing to guard is now up for grabs. I head upstairs, confused about what I should do—talk to the Lord or entertain thoughts of the pool, the radio, the moment of lustful bliss on the television. Lying in bed I open up my Bible and turn to a passage. After reading a couple verses, the excitement of lust returns. Dwelling on those thoughts I fall into the fast track of the road to masturbation.

"I lie there in my bed confused and wondering what went wrong and one thought comes to mind: I am not satisfied and I am guilty."

Why does Adam feel guilty? Because masturbation is sin. In every sense of the word, masturbation is a sin. I need to be very clear about this right up front. Most Christians agree that fornication and pornography are sins. There is not such agreement on the area of masturbation.

An Act of Personal Preference?

Some might argue that because the words "masturbation is sin" are not in the Bible, Christians may practice this activity according to their own personal preference. Some say that they can masturbate without lusting. They feel no conviction for the act. I would like to engage these views, and show from God's Word where their reasoning just doesn't add up.

Masturbation is an act born of and infested with lustful thoughts. In Philippians 4:8, Paul tells us, "Finally, brothers, whatever is true, whatever is noble, whatever is right, whatever is pure, whatever is lovely, whatever is admirable —if anything is excellent or praiseworthy—think about such things." These are certainly not words that describe a guy's thoughts while he masturbates. Further, Jesus said, "Anyone who looks at a woman lustfully has already committed adultery with her in his heart" (Matthew 5:28).

"But I don't think lustfully about girls when I masturbate," you might say. "I just have to because I have so much natural sexual tension built up." Let me ask you why is so much sexual tension building up in the first place? I know that whenever I would fall into masturbation late at night, that was *never* the beginning of the sin. Rather, the sinful act at the end of the day was simply the inevitable conclusion of an entire day filled to the brim with carnal thoughts, stares, and daydreams. Most guys will admit the lustful thoughts led to sexual tension that led to sexual arousal and the belief that one needs physical release.

My friend Jeff told me this analogy. Think of masturbation as a Super Soaker 50 water gun. You know, the kind that you pump full of pressure so the water comes out when you pull the trigger. When you look at women with lust throughout the day it's like you are pumping that Super Soaker 50 full of pressure. Your mind is ready to explode with thoughts. Then, when night falls and you are going to bed, all Satan has to do is pull the trigger of temptation and you fall into masturbation. But if, throughout the day, you are not lusting, there is no pressure built up. So when Satan pulls the trigger of temptation, nothing happens. You have no sexual tension to be rid of. You will be truly amazed by the difference in your body's hormones when you begin refraining from sin at the beginning of the day, instead of lusting all day long, and then suddenly deciding to be holy when you know you're about to do the thing that makes you feel so dirty and guilty.

Of course, it doesn't take all day for guys to become aroused—for many guys it only takes a quick, steamy scene in a movie, for instance, and their hormones are going wild. Because guys are attracted visually to women, a guy can be aroused quickly. An erection may be a reaction, but the physical response *will* pass, and a guy doesn't have to indulge the feeling or stimulate it.

Natural Release

It is true that guys constantly produce sperm and semen, and that it needs to be released somehow. This is a major argument for masturbation. But God, in His sovereign provision for us, has made a way for that semen to be released naturally, without conjuring up the lustful thoughts that masturbation involves. God has given us *nocturnal emission,* also known as "wet dreams." When you stop masturbating, your body will naturally relieve itself in your sleep, without needing any lustful thoughts or help from you. This is perfectly safe and natural, and it works.

Selfish and Unsatisfying

Masturbation is also entirely selfish. Eldredge says, "Masturbation is sabotage. It is an inherently selfish act that tears you down. I've spoken with many men whose addiction to masturbation has eroded their sense of strength."[1] God gave us the gift of sexuality as an expression of love and service to our wives—there is nothing loving or selfless about masturbation. This also explains why masturbation is never truly satisfying. Dr. Mark Laaser explains: "Masturbation . . . is never ultimately satisfying because it falls short of the incredibly satisfying nature of a spiritual union with a wife."[2]

The Temple of the Holy Spirit

"Flee from sexual immorality. All other sins a man commits are outside the body, but he who sins sexually sins against his own body. . . . Your body is a temple of the Holy Spirit. . . . Therefore honor God with your body," the Scripture declares (1 Corinthians 6:18–20). When you masturbate, do you feel that you are honoring God with your body, or are you sinning against your own body? Are you full of thoughts of regret and conviction? The Bible says, "It is sin to know what you ought to do and then not do it" (James 4:17 NLT). Masturbation is something that I always knew was wrong, even though no one ever told me so. My parents never warned me about it, and my friends only encouraged it. Yet somehow I always knew that it was wrong.

Here are two questions to ask yourself if you masturbate: Is your masturbation associated with lustful thoughts of flesh and carnality? Does the act produce feelings of guilt and shame, so that you can't seem to face anyone after you do it? Our Lord God wants an intimate relationship; such a relationship cannot be realized while we continue to wallow in a selfish, sinful practice. All sexual sin, including lust, fornication, and masturbation, is wrong. If you agree with me and want to be rid of all of it, look with me into God's Word and see what it has to say for our struggle.

This chapter is full of strategies to help you overcome these temptations, but for any of these approaches to succeed in your life, you must first be willing to admit that the acts are wrong. If you don't, you'll never change. As Jesus said, "I have come to call the sick, not those who think they are healthy."

Let's Go to War

This issue is more difficult to deal with, I'll admit, but we can still have victory over masturbation! Almost every single guy struggles or has struggled with this. There may be some guys who haven't, but they're few and far between. A 2004 study entitled "Faith Matters: Teenagers, Sexuality, and Religion" surveyed more than 5,800 teenagers involved in faith-based institutions and found that 89 percent of males in the eleventh and twelfth grades masturbate.[3] This doesn't even tell how many guys have *ever* masturbated, and the older they get, the higher the numbers are. Most guys get involved with masturbation sometime between ages ten and fourteen; for many of them, the struggle continues for the rest of their life. Even when they get married and have a healthy sex life with their wife, they still masturbate because *no woman in the world has the sex drive of a man!* If they did, then we'd never get anything done around here.

Why is this sin so rampant? Because we take everything we need to do it everywhere we go! There is no "tourniquet" step with this one. Sorry, brother, but we're going to have to stick with bandages on this one, because we really need this limb! But don't lose heart; there is hope. In fact, a major motivation for writing this book was my own victory over masturbation, not just pornography. I'm a guy who used to masturbate nearly every day—sometimes more. I've struggled from the age of eleven. I haven't completely gotten rid of it yet, but I've gone from every day to just a couple of times in the last two and a half years! The change has been wonderful. That's one reason I'm writing this book: I want every one of my brothers in Christ to experience the same victory.

Steps to Break the Habit

Here are six practical steps for any Christian guy to take.

First, *gain victory over sexual sin*—with girls and with pornography. Masturbation can happen without either a girl or pornography in your life, but if you don't master the temptations that each brings, you'll have almost no chance of overcoming masturbation. This is especially true if you're in a relationship with a girl where you don't have sex, but you constantly lust after her and push the boundaries. When you go home afterward, you may masturbate or face the temptation to do so. Recognize that the activity still screams "sex outside of marriage."

For me, the struggle with masturbation virtually vanished when I stopped looking at pornography. This might be the same for you, but even if it's not, it's still a great start.

The second step is to *know when and where you struggle,* and build a bigger defense for those times. After step one, this one is key.

Do you usually masturbate late at night? Then go to bed earlier and spend quality time with the Lord before bed in prayer and Bible study or memory. Do you usually masturbate in the shower? Then stop taking showers. (Just kidding.) If you masturbate in the shower, then memorize Scripture and recite it the whole time you're in the shower, or sing your favorite hymns or praise songs in the shower.

This is why your battle plan needs to be unique, because only you know when you're most vulnerable to temptation.

The third step is to *plan your discretionary time and know when you're going to be alone.* This one goes hand in hand with step two. One big stimulus for masturbation is stress, but another is boredom. Plan to fill free time with emotionally, mentally, and physically stimulating activities. As one friend said, "Read good books, talk to God, get a job, work out, go hang out with friends, write a letter. Boredom allows space for temptation."

Fourth, *commit to regular physical exercise.* Lack of physical exercise is a major contributor to the struggle for a lot of guys, so we should make exercise an important part of our schedule; we can do a little more of it when we're feeling especially tempted. Going for a run or lifting weights is a great, productive way to spend that extra energy. Physical exercise can help in your struggle with masturbation and other sexual sin because it actually helps to balance your hormones and chemicals in your body, and it can make you feel better about yourself in general.

Fifth, *go to the bathroom.* Many times when we have the urge to masturbate, our bladder is just full and it needs to be emptied. Next time you have the urge to masturbate, try taking a pee.

Sixth, *go to bed.* Many guys masturbate because it's either late at night, they're extremely tired, or both. Brother, we need every bit of energy that we can get to battle sexual sin, especially temptations that will always be here—like the one to masturbate—so we do ourselves a million favors by just turning in. If you have to study or get some work done, try going to bed and waking up early. Our brains work better in the morning anyhow—which is why we go to school then.

Next to our desire to lust, there is no other sexual temptation that will be harder to rid ourselves of than masturbation. But be encouraged that it is something that can be overcome. Decide today that masturbation is a sin, and don't fool yourself by pretending it's not, or that you're powerless in its clutches. Remember to help yourself out by running from lust throughout the day, and running to the Lord when you're exasperated with life rather than to masturbation.

REFLECTIONS

1. *How do you feel when you masturbate? Do you agree with the author that it is sin? Why or why not?*

2. *Develop a battle plan today for how you will avoid the temptation to masturbate, and share that with a trusted friend or mentor.*

> The ways of a woman's heart are mysterious and deep, and they run over with emotion. To try to understand her is impossible, but to capture and protect her heart is valiant, the call of a true warrior who fights to the bloody end to protect the one he loves.
>
> **LYSA TerKEURST**
> *Capture Her Heart*

Love is patient, love is kind. It does not envy, it does not boast, it is not proud. It is not rude, it is not self-seeking, it is not easily angered, it keeps no record of wrongs. Love does not delight in evil but rejoices with the truth. It always protects, always trusts, always hopes, always perseveres. Love never fails.

1 Corinthians 13:4–8

CHAPTER 10

Treat Her Right

BRIAN Bales (not his real name) was as good a guy as they come. He was active in school and church, and respected by everyone who knew him. Even though he has been one of my best friends for years, I never knew everything he was going through, until recently. He shared this story with me about a relationship that formed during his senior year of high school.

When Sarah and I started dating, we both changed. We began hanging out alone at her house after school and on weekends. Though we studied the Bible together, it was just a cover-up for what we really wanted to do. Often we would sit in my car or on a couch or on her bed and make out. At first it was just a prolonged kiss. Then my hands would go a little lower. Then I would feel guilty and we would ask for forgiveness and I would be determined to change. The next time we would PUT ourselves in the same situation and go a little further. This progression continued, with each of our heavenly relationships growing old and stale. One of the hardest things for me was that Sarah completely put the physical aspect of the relationship in my hands. She never stopped me and even sometimes provoked me to go further. Eventually, it became a weekly thing.

One night will be forever ingrained in my mind. I was spending the night after a day with her family at Kelly's Island. We were going to go to her church the next morning. That night we went the furthest we ever went. We kept going and going, desiring to satisfy our lust for each other, and yet, the further we went the more we wanted. We finally moved from the living room up to her room where we made out, and came so close to going all the way that it scared me half to death. We finally realized what we were doing, and without saying a word, we just stopped and went to bed (separately). The next day, ironically enough, church was about premarital sex. God's got a pretty funny sense of humor.

Later, during a summer conference in Colorado, I realized that Sarah and I had nothing in common except for a desire to have sex. I knew God was calling me to break off the relationship for several reasons. Sarah was not committed to serving the Lord, but more important, I was not mature enough in my faith right then to be leading a relationship. I did not have my armor on and I knew very few of the tactics for fighting sexual temptation. I felt as if my name were Judas Iscariot. I had given everyone around me the impression that I desired to know God more and more each day. The truth was I desired to go further and further with Sarah every day.

"The love life of a Christian is a crucial battleground," wrote Elisabeth Elliot in *Passion and Purity*. "There, if nowhere else, it will be determined as to who is Lord: the world, the self and the devil, or the Lord Christ."

Paul told Timothy, "Treat . . . younger women as sisters, with absolute purity" (1 Timothy 5:1–2). If you've ever read the Song of Solomon, you start to get the idea that men are supposed to be leaders in purity and holiness and in relationships with the opposite sex. Under no circumstance are we allowed to have sexual intercourse or do anything else sexual with our girlfriend or with any girl who is not *currently* our wife.

Yes, that means that we cannot have sex with our fiancée! I have a lot of friends who are engaged, and from what I hear that is the toughest time of all. But those friends are waiting until their wedding night for the same reason that I'm waiting now: because we know that God has commanded it and we know that we will enjoy sex so much more when it is done within God's set parameters. God has the most abundant life possible for us if we obey His commands. This promise extends to sex as well.

Worth the Wait

I asked several married friends if they waited to have sex until they were married, and if they did, if it was worth it. For those of them that waited, the unanimous answer was a resounding "Yes!" Here's what a couple of them said:

> Yes, I waited; it was totally worth it and you will never regret saving it for marriage.
>
> *John*

> Yes, I waited for my wife . . . and it was definitely worth it! A woman's primary need in the marriage relationship is security. Having saved sex for marriage, I was able to give my wife the

security of knowing that she is not being compared to anyone else. This has been one of the best gifts that I have been able to give to my wife!

Rob

One of my best friends just got married this summer, and he included this in an e-mail just recently:

P.S. Waiting for the right girl is worth it!!! Emily is a wonderful and amazing wife and it is my joy to know, love and cherish her— thought this would encourage you to keep trusting in Him to provide in His time.

Jacob

If you have never had sex outside marriage, then I admonish you with all my heart to make a firm commitment to keep your virginity until your wedding night. But if you have already committed fornication, or even adultery, don't lose heart. A couple of close friends of mine moved in with each other while they were dating, but they became convicted and moved out. They were engaged soon afterward. Their marriage has been going strong for years now, and they are still deeply in love! There is still as much hope for you as there is for me or for any guy! I don't say this just as a concession, and you don't have to take my word for it. Remember, Jesus Himself told us that every guy on earth has sinned as badly as you have (see Matthew 5:28). The only guy you'll ever find who isn't guilty of adultery (through lusting) is a guy who has never seen a girl!

Don't lose heart, dear brother; I am firmly convinced that you can be restored to fellowship with Christ and you can live just as fruitful a life as any man can, including being just as good a husband and father as anyone else. Believe that, and don't ever let anyone tell you any different.

This is also an important point for those of you who may not have fallen into fornication to consider. Maybe because you have abstained from actually getting in bed with a girl, you think that you're somehow higher and mightier than one who has slept with his girlfriend, even though you have lusted and masturbated countless times. Jesus would call you a hypocrite. Don't get me wrong; I commend you for taking that stand and for saving yourself for marriage until now, and I encourage you to continue by the power and help of the Lord Jesus Christ. But it is important for you to realize that in God's eyes, by committing adultery through lustful thoughts you are every bit as much a sinner as the guy who has fallen into sexual sin in his relationships with girls. Why is it so important? Check this out: "So, if you think you are standing firm, be careful that you don't fall" (1 Corinthians 10:12). If you think you're beyond these other sins, then Satan may be tricking you into falling right into them!

I have a friend who has slept with several women, and he and I were talking about sin one day. Although I had never said it or even implied it, he was under the impression I thought that because he had slept around and I had maintained my virginity, I was somehow less of a sinner than he. Not only do I not think that, I told him the Bible confirms that it is not true. I showed him Jesus' statement in Matthew 5:28, and I explained how the sin that I have already committed was by itself severe enough to earn me eternal damnation in hell. He understood, and it meant a lot to him to know that he was no worse than me in the eyes of God.

Key Strategies for Staying Pure

So whether you're a virgin or you've just recommitted to abstinence today, here is a list of strategies that will help you to be sexually pure when you're with one of God's daughters.

Strategy 1: Clean Out the Gutters of Your Mind and Heart

Much of this has been said already, but it's important to include here as the first strategy to avoid sexual sin with a girl. If you are heavily involved with any of the sinful practices mentioned in chapters 7 through 9, you will inevitably visualize those experiences and, if they continue, eventually try to act them out with a girl. I have never personally viewed pornography while I was dating a girl, but I've heard from a lot of other guys that when you do you visualize the things that you saw in those magazines, Web sites, or videos when you are with your date. If it's lust or masturbation you're involved with, your heart will want some sort of sexual gratification from that girl since you were craving it in your mind so much all day. Brother, we've got to clean out our minds and hearts before we can ever treat one of God's daughters the way that He would have us treat her.

Strategy 2: Set Clear, Unbreakable Boundaries

We must plan ahead, before the date, by setting clear boundaries and then tell another person about them, so we can be accountable.

This is part of the Battle Plan. This is something I've learned, and it's true for every single guy I've ever talked to: when we're facing temptation, we're going to get as close to the line as we've allowed ourselves to ahead of time. If we haven't decided whether we're going to let ourselves watch R-rated movies ahead of time, we're not going to choose not to when we're out with our friends and they are asking us to join them. The same is true when we're out with a girl. If we haven't decided if we're going to kiss her, and she'll let us kiss her, then we're going to kiss her! The same is true with every other step in the progression toward sexual intercourse.

While you're setting your boundaries, keep in mind that it's not just sexual intercourse that we are commanded to avoid; it is anything sexual or anything that would arouse sexual thoughts. Have your mom help you develop your boundaries. Or better yet, have your girlfriend's dad help you.

When I set my boundaries, I want to do absolutely nothing that should be saved for my wife. I have already done things with a girl that I should have waited until marriage to do, but those sins are in the past and *I am not going to lower my standard of purity because I foolishly lowered it one time years ago!* By the grace of God I'm going to be able to tell my wife that she's the first person I've even had sex with, and I can also tell her that she's the first person I've kissed or done anything more with since high school. She's going to appreciate that a whole lot more than if I have to tell her that I've sinned with a dozen different girls in the years since then!

Set your boundaries high. Bob Gresh has noted ten steps in sexual activity that lead to sexual intercourse; look at the chart showing the steps (next page). If we can't decide between two of these levels for our boundary, Bob's rule of thumb is to go with the higher one. The comments in italics are also Bob's.

When setting our boundaries, we've got to ask the questions "What does the Lord want me to do?" and "How can I be a leader in purity in this relationship?" instead of "What can I get away with?" If the question on our mind is the last one, then we're going to sin, even if only in our mind.

Progression to Sexual Activity	
Step 1.	Looking at a girl and making eye contact (*Remember, we are visually stimulated.*)
Step 2.	Talking with a girl (*Hey, ever notice how much passion talk can create?*)
Step 3.	Holding hands (*This can be a nice sign of attachment.*)
Step 4.	Hands on shoulders and hands on waist (*Can you handle this? Can she?*)
Step 5.	Kissing on the cheek or softly kissing on the lips (*This is a sweet, innocent kiss.*)
Step 6.	Open-mouthed passionate kissing (*A new desire awakens.*)
Step 7.	Petting while clothed
Step 8.	Experimental nakedness
Step 9.	Oral sex
Step 10.	Sexual intercourse

SOURCE: Adapted from Bob Gresh, *Who Moved the Goalpost?* (Chicago: Moody, 2001), 133.

Take an honest look at that list, and ask yourself which of those things should only be done with our wife. I am not going to do anything in numbers 6–10 until my wedding night, and I'm going to be extremely careful about numbers 3–5 as well. And just think of the reward! The day I get to do number 6 is the same day I get to do numbers 7–10. I think I'll pass out in the middle of the wedding from the thought!

My good friend Mike shares the following story that illustrates how the boundaries may vary, depending on you and the woman you date:

When Melissa and I started dating, we got off on the wrong foot. I was weak in my faith and strong in my hormones and our first date included our first kiss. Kissing was a big part of our relationship early on, and we enjoyed spending as much time as we could alone. This got dangerous after a while, and we found ourselves pushing the limits of our loosely defined standards and trying to find something in the Scriptures that would allow us to do whatever we wanted as long as we didn't have sex. Thankfully, God spared us from doing much more than kissing, but when I think about how close we came to crossing that line it scares me.

Somewhere around the end of our first year of dating, we realized how selfish we were being. We were stepping out of God's plan and twisting the Scriptures to justify it. We decided that we needed to take a week away from each other to evaluate our relationship, mostly the physical part of it. That week was one of the hardest of my life and I feared that Melissa and I would decide to end our relationship in order to stay pure. But, after a week of prayer, we went out to eat together and both came to the same conclusion—we would no longer kiss until we were married, and we would not hold hands until we were engaged. Being physical at all was just too dangerous for us, so we decided to cut it out. We were afraid that our intimacy would take a few steps back, but God surprised us. We grew closer after that decision than we had ever been before.

The past three years without a physical relationship have been difficult. But I know that they paved the way for an amazing, intimate relationship that would not have been possible had we not submitted to God's design. On July 4, 2003, I took Melissa's hand for the "first" time as I slipped the engagement ring on her finger under the fireworks. I can't wait until this August 14 when I can hold her in my arms and kiss her for the "first" time as my beautiful bride.

I just recently got this update from Mike:

On August 14, 2004, I truly realized how important our decision for purity was. As I watched my beautiful bride walk down the aisle in her white dress, in her purity, I couldn't keep from crying. This was the moment I waited for. This was why we made our decision. This was God's gift to me: my helper, my best friend, my bride. It was so significant for the pastor to tell me to kiss my bride because I hadn't for so long. As we slipped into each other's arms and took our "first" kiss, we knew that it was worth the wait. It may seem silly in our culture to avoid a physical relationship, but you have to believe that God's plan is better and honored far beyond our own. At our reception, the whole room went into applause as my best man reminded them of our decision to wait. We were congratulated, honored, and respected for our tough decision.

Strategy 3: Plan Your Date, Avoid Tempting Places, and Set a Return Time

The third strategy is to plan your date ahead of time, avoid tempting places, and set a time to have her back home. The reason for this goes back to the reason for the last one. We have to plan ahead because we're not going to make the best choices on the date when we're with the girl. Avoid places where couples are known to get alone and make out. You might even decide that you're not going to go anywhere totally alone while you're dating. Such choices may cause some inconvenience, but we must be willing to be a little inconvenienced for the sake of purity.

Then tell her and her parents (if she lives at home) where you're going and when you're going to have her home, and be true to your word. If you're delayed beyond your control, call her house and let her parents know. Doing these things will help keep you out of a lot of trouble—and it will honor her parents.

This won't always work in every situation. If your girlfriend lives far from her parents, it may not be possible to tell them every time you go out together. If this is the case, then it's a good idea to tell friends or a mentor where you're going and when you'll be back, and ask them to hold you accountable to it when you return. Accountability is not as easy when she doesn't live at home, but it's so important to do to protect her purity and your own.

Strategy 4: When in Trouble, *Run!*

Sometimes it's not just the guy who is pushing the girl to go further. Sometimes it's her. Many times you can avoid this by being very picky about the type of girl you take out, but not always. If she's tempting you to sin with her, leave. Take her home. Get out of there! Remember, that was Joseph's approach when Potiphar's wife was coming on to him (see chapter 7).

So if you need to, run! You may feel or look foolish at the time, but you'll thank yourself later on—and so will your future wife.

Strategy 5: Be Careful Where You Pray with Her

"The couple that prays together lays together." The first time I heard this I had the same skeptical look on my face that you're now wearing all of a sudden. I didn't understand what it meant either, but my friend Joe Williams explained it to me. Joe graduated from college in 1997 and is now married, but he learned this while he was still in college. He actually knew of a few couples who set out to pray but ended up having sex *that same night*. I do think that couples ought to pray together, but the couple needs to be careful about where they pray, because it can draw two people into an uncontrollable level of intimacy.

That being said, I do want to stress how beneficial prayer can be in dating. For years I've only dated girls I could pray with; I have no business in a romantic relationship with a girl I can't pray with. Pastor Randy Pope, author of *Finding Your Million Dollar Mate,* felt the same way when he was dating: "I made a vow to the Lord that I would never go out with any girl if I could not pray freely with her on a date."[1] I plan to pray with my girlfriend a lot, but because of this warning I'm going to examine my heart before I do, and be careful where and when I do so.

Strategy 6: Live Blamelessly!

This one sort of ties together all the rest, and it's probably the most important piece of advice I've ever received in regard to dating. We should have both Christian and non-Christian friends, but the Bible tells us we should only pursue Christian women romantically (see 2 Corinthians 6:14). If we do date, we must remember that every Christian woman is one of God's daughters, and we should strive to see her and treat her as a daughter of God. We should have no regrets at the end of the day when we return that young lady to her dad and her Father.

I want to be able to shake that father's hand, look him straight in the eye, and tell him, "Sir, I've treated your daughter with the utmost respect. There is nothing I have done on our date that would make you angry with me. I've kept your daughter pure, and I've taken nothing from her that didn't belong to me. Thank you for the privilege of spending time with such a precious lady. She's God's daughter, and she's your daughter, and I'll always keep that in mind."

Strategy 7: Apply the Tourniquet

If all else fails, or if you know that the relationship is not honoring the Lord and not edifying one or both of you, apply the tourniquet. Break off the relationship. If she's causing you to sin, then she's probably not the woman that you want to be your wife. If you're causing her to sin, then you probably need to get out, at least for now, until you can get yourself under control and have Christ do some major surgery on your heart and mind.

This is not going to be easy; it might be one of the most difficult things that you ever do, but if that's what you need to do, then do it. Once again, your future wife will be so grateful that you did.

Remember my friend Brian Bales, introduced in this chapter? After breaking up with Sarah, he took some time off from the dating scene and went solo with God awhile. About a year later, he met a great girl named Karen, but he waited to start dating until they had built a strong friendship.

Now they've been dating for over two years, and their relationship is marked with purity and centered on Christ. Last week, Brian asked Karen to marry him, and she said yes! Their relationship is an inspiration to me and to all of their friends. Brian shares how he's been able to have victory in this new relationship:

> I have found in my relationship with Karen that one of the most important aspects of sexual purity in a relationship is setting boundaries *together!* If you just set boundaries by yourself, there is no one to keep you accountable. . . . I have also found in my relationship with Karen that because of my sexually impure past, we must make much tighter boundaries than another couple who have never fallen into sexual sin. For example, if I were to kiss Karen I would not be able to stop, but this is not true with some couples.
>
> It is also important in a relationship to be open about what the other individual does that may lead you into sexual impurity.

Karen may wear a seemingly modest shirt. However, because I am 14 inches taller than she is, if I'm within two feet of her, I can see right down her shirt. I like that, which means I must ask her to put on a sweatshirt or button-up shirt that allows me no opportunity to let my mind wander. Granted, even if she was wearing an Eskimo suit, I could picture her in a bikini, but you gotta help yourself out. You can't ask God to save you from an oncoming semi truck and then step out in front of it just as it is getting ready to pass.

REFLECTIONS

1. *If you're in a relationship right now, how's it going? Do you need to adjust your boundaries or even apply the tourniquet, or just press on with the boundaries you've already set up?*

2. *Are you harboring any guilt and condemnation from past sins you've already repented of and Christ has already forgiven? If so, take those to the Lord and let Him heal you today.*

" We Christian men need each other. There is strength in numbers. When isolated and separated from our brothers, we are easy pickings for the enemy of our souls.

ROBERT DANIELS
The War Within

As iron sharpens iron, so one man sharpens another.
Proverbs 27:17

CHAPTER 11

A Band
of Brothers

D O you know a guy who really wants to grow in Christ and wants to reach his full potential for serving the Lord and others? Then there are two vitally important relationships I urge him to become involved in. The first is a relationship with another guy close to his own age whom he can confide in. The two of them will keep each other accountable, praying for and encouraging each other and spurring each other on. The second relationship is one with an older brother in Christ whom he can look up to for wisdom and guidance, who will teach him things from experience that someone his own age couldn't.

Both of these relationships fall into the area of *accountability,* and you'll be amazed at the powerful impact that each of these relationships can have on every aspect of your life, especially in the area of sexual integrity and holiness.

Accountability has been one of the most powerful and effective tools that the Lord has used in my life to bring real and lasting change in many of my sinful struggles. Besides prayer and Scripture memorization, accountability has been the number one tool to overcome sexual temptation among all of the guys I have interviewed.

In his book *Knowing God,* J. I. Packer said that aside from the written Word of God, God communicates with us in no clearer way than by other trusted Christians. The book of Ecclesiastes tells us that "two are better than one. . . . If one falls down, his friend can help him up. But pity the man who falls and has no one to help him up! . . . Though one may be overpowered, two can defend themselves. A cord of three strands is not quickly broken" (4:9, 10, 12). The work that our God can do when just two guys come together in the name of the Lord is just awesome.

By the way, this accountability partner definitely needs to be another guy. We should never confide in a female friend of ours with all of our sexual struggles. That's more responsibility than any girl should have, and it will only create a very uncomfortable and potentially dangerous relationship. Once married, the relationship changes; as a man chooses to confide in his wife, the woman may turn out to be his very best accountability partner. But while single, don't confide in a female friend. That's an extremely bad idea. Find a good Christian guy to be your accountability partner.

A Matter of Terms

Some people get hung up on the word *accountability,* as they associate it with something weak and worthless. This sort of meeting can be just that, if you get together with guys who are weak and will be content to wallow in defeat week after week, meeting just to normalize their sin. Don't make this kind of guy your partner, and don't have this kind of meeting. You can call the relationship whatever you like, such as "Band of Brothers," "Teammates" (as Bob Gresh calls it), or "Battle Partners" (as Robert Daniels refers to it in *The War Within*). You may even call it "WAR—Warriors Avowing Revolution." I call it accountability because that's what I've always called it, and it's neither weak nor worthless, because I've seen it produce significant changes in my life and in my heart. Be intentional about the purpose and goals behind your meeting, and don't get hung up with terms.

How Embarrassing!

You might be thinking all of this sounds rather embarrassing. *How could I possibly get together and talk about the things that I struggle with, especially really uncomfortable things like masturbation, lust, pornography, or fooling around with a girlfriend?* Your concern is a valid one, but it's one to be overcome. The embarrassing thing is really when you think you're alone. Once you break the ice, all of these things are much easier to deal with.

Here's what one college freshman said about accountability: "You're not alone!! When I was younger, I felt so alone. I thought I was the only one who struggled with this, and I was so embarrassed. Realize that every other guy has these same problems, and there are older guys who will help you. We are all brothers; there's no need to be embarrassed. We have to back each other up."

He's certainly not the only one who's found the power of accountability to make a difference in his life. In his book *The Search for Significance,* Robert McGee says, "It is difficult—if not impossible—to turn on the light of objectivity by ourselves. We need guidance from the Holy Spirit, *as well as the honesty, love, and encouragement of at least one other person who's willing to help us.*"[1]

Being Accountable: Sam and Joe

My first accountability partner was Sam Richard. I met him the summer before my sophomore year in high school, shortly after I had committed my life to the Lord Jesus. Sam and I were both fifteen years old, and this was the first accountability experience for each of us. We met at church and were encouraged to start this accountability time by our youth pastor, Stephen Bauer. Because we went to different schools and could not drive, Sam and I didn't always get to meet every single week. But we never quit, and if we had to miss a week's meeting for whatever reason, we would be right back there the next week to meet again.

Sam and I continued to meet throughout high school until we both graduated in the spring of 2001 and went off to different colleges. We've remained good friends to this day, and we still keep tabs on each other to see how we're both doing, especially in the area of sexual purity.

It was through accountability with Sam that I had my first real victories over sexual sin. It broke my heart to have to tell Sam that I had messed up. Because of that, many times I wouldn't masturbate or commit a number of other sins because I knew I'd have to tell Sam all about it the next time we met.

Accountability is like turning on a light in a very dark room. Often we can almost compartmentalize our lives, putting the things that we do in front of people over here in this life, and putting the things that we do when we're alone over there in another life. That's no way to live; that's hypocrisy. Moses wrote in Psalm 90:8, "You have set our iniquities before you, our secret sins in the light of your presence."

When I went off to college, I met Joe Schneider in Air Force ROTC; we hit it off right away. Sam and I were both praying that the Lord would show us each another guy at our respective colleges who would keep us accountable, like we had done for each other in high school. Through a lot of prayer and time spent with Joe, I knew that he was the new guy for the job.

Joe and I did a really interesting thing during our sophomore year; we decided to room together. Many people warned me that you should never room with one of your best buddies, because you might grow to hate each other. But I thought that was ridiculous, so we went for it. I wanted the challenge. Besides, I expect that my best friend in life is going to be my wife, and if I hope to live with her later on, then I'd better be able to coexist with Joe now.

Rooming with my accountability partner turned out to be the very best thing for me. I told him right away about my freshman year struggle with pornography and my longtime battle with masturbation. It provided a huge degree of accountability to have him there with me every day, able to check up on me and confront me if I would do anything suspicious. Like I said, I didn't fall into pornography for an entire semester, and that was largely because of Joe.

Joe and I didn't room together last year, but we still got together every week for prayer and accountability. This year, our last year in college, we're rooming together once again. I thank God for both Sam and Joe and for the work He's done in my life because of these two men of God.

Those Accountability Meetings

I encourage you to set a regular meeting time and place and stick to it. Since I started meeting with my first accountability partner six years ago, I have made an effort to meet with him once a week, every week. This is critical, because if we don't set a regular meeting time and place, we will forget about it, put it off, and then we'll never do it.

Along with this, there are five elements that need to be part of our accountability relationship, which come straight from Scripture. They are as follows:

1. Prayer

Jesus said, "If two of you on earth agree on anything you ask for, it will be done for you by my Father in heaven. For where two or three come together in my name, there am I with them" (Matthew 18:19–20). The apostle James added: "The prayer of a righteous man is powerful and effective" (James 5:16). Open and close your meetings with prayer. By praying we commit the meeting to the Lord and set the focus on Him.

2. Confession

"Therefore confess your sins to each other and pray for each other so that you might be healed" (James 5:16). By confessing to each other we are held accountable for our actions, even the ones that might not have produced any immediate earthly consequence. My vision for accountability is this: Every time we remember that we have to give an account for our actions to our accountability partner, we will remember that the perfect, holy God is watching us, and we will have to give an account to Him when we stand before Him at the judgment seat of Christ.

3. Encouragement and burden-bearing

"See to it, brothers, that none of you has a sinful, unbelieving heart that turns away from the living God. But *encourage one another daily . . . so that none of you may be hardened by sin's deceitfulness*" (Hebrews 3:12–13, emphasis added). God has made us relational people, and He has made us to be most fulfilled when we are serving others, and most emotionally healthy when we can share the load of our own burdens with someone else as well. As Paul wrote, "Carry each other's burdens, and in this way you will fulfill the law of Christ" (Galatians 6:2).

4. Chastisement

"Wounds from a friend can be trusted, but an enemy multiplies kisses" (Proverbs 27:6). There is a delicate balance between being an *encourager* and a *flatterer*. We are all commanded to be the first, but we are also commanded not to be the second. A pastor once told me that the difference between the two is in the motive of our heart. Do we say things so that people will like us and feel good about themselves, or do we encourage them with the truth, telling them that we love them and that we see the Lord at work in and through their life, but also that there are some areas we see in them that need to change?

5. Spurring one another on

"Let us hold unswervingly to the hope we profess, for he who promised is faithful. And *let us consider how we may spur one another on* toward love and good deeds. Let us not give up meeting together, as some are in the habit of doing, but let us encourage one another—and all the more as you see the Day approaching" (Hebrews 10:23–25, emphasis added). Finally, let's make this relationship one where we become more *useful* to God because of it. Let's not only bear each other's burdens and challenge each other not to sin, but let's "spur one another on toward love and good deeds" as well!

The Other Critically Important Relationship: Having a Mentor

An accountability relationship with another guy near your age is only one of the two accountability relationships that can change your life in this area. The other is having a mentor. Ask the Lord to show you a man whom you trust and look up to who would be able to help you in this area and all areas of your life. When the Lord shows you such a man, ask him if he would be willing to meet with you to disciple you, much as Paul discipled Timothy.

I know that asking someone to do this is not an easy thing to, and be warned that the first man you ask may not be able to meet with you. He may be overcommitted already and he won't feel that he can do the relationship justice. Please don't give up, though. Try again. It will be so worth it when you finally get in that relationship and see what God has in store for you.

I have had a greater number of mentors in my life than accountability partners. Perhaps I just need more than one man to teach me and keep me in line! My first formal mentor was my youth pastor, David Life. Just before my junior year of high school, he asked me if I was being discipled. When I told him I wasn't, he asked if I'd like to set up a weekly time when the two of us could meet and grow in the Lord together. Naturally, he didn't share his struggles with me to the level that I did with him, but he did share prayer concerns and other challenges with me, and together the Lord worked in both of our lives.

That year of discipleship was highlighted at the end when the two of us went on a missions trip together to an orphanage in Tijuana, Mexico. It was my first foreign missions trip and in fact the first time I had ever ridden in a plane. This was one of the best weeks of my life, and I was glad to share it with Pastor Dave.

Throughout high school, my senior pastor, Bob Hudberg, and my football coach and guidance counselor, Ryan Teglovic, were also instrumental in discipling me as well, even though we never had a regular meeting time.

When I got to college the Lord provided Lt. Col. Bert Fujishige, USAF (retired), and Pastor Bob Rohm to fill the mentor bill in my life. It's been awesome to see the consistency of character in the men that God has brought my way. Since then the Lord has also provided me with Brad Smith, Jim Amstutz, and Dr. Bill Brown to disciple me at different times and in different situations as well. It seems that the Lord never allows me to grow too attached to any one man. I can only assume that this is because He wants to always remind me that it is He and He alone who produces any lasting change in my life. These godly men are simply the instruments that He often uses to facilitate that change, but the source of the change is always the Lord.

This mentoring relationship can take many forms, but a

great way to start is a weekly meeting like the one we described with accountability. Some mentors like to work through a book with their "mentee," to serve as a springboard for their weekly discussions.[2] You may want to meet for breakfast or lunch, or do some activity together that you both enjoy, or you may just want to meet in his office or home.

One final admonition: Please don't put off seeking these relationships for too long; you just don't know what you're missing that the Lord has in store for you through them! May God bless you as you prayerfully consider whom you should ask to be an accountability partner and who should be your mentor.

REFLECTIONS

1. *Do you have an accountability partner and a mentor whom you meet with regularly? If not, write down some names of guys your age that could be your accountability partner, and then some names of guys who could serve as your mentor; pray about which ones you should approach to ask about it.*

2. *What specific goals do you have for accountability? Along with purity, what areas of your life would you like to work on with your accountability partner or your mentor? Write these down and share them with him at your next meeting.*

❝ Sin will not spare for one day. There is no safety but in constant warfare for those who desire deliverance from sin's perplexing rebellion.

JOHN OWEN,
The Mortification of Sin

So, if you think you are standing firm, be careful that you don't fall!

1 Corinthians 10:12

CHAPTER 12

Sprinting the Marathon

SOMETHING hit home the day I wrote that journal entry in chapter 2. I had been running the race looking for the solution, "the easy answer that will rid me of this devastating struggle and make me forever perfectly pure." I thought I was a sprinter finishing a 100-yard dash, and I was grasping desperately for the finish line—but I was in the *wrong race!*

The battle for sexual purity isn't a quick sprint; it's a long-fought marathon and the finish line arrives the day we go to be with Christ. No one ever finished a marathon who was running it like a sprint. So I needed to take off my sprinting shoes, put on my distance shoes, and gear up for the long haul.

By applying the lessons that the Lord has taught me about purity and holiness, I'm now winning the early stages of this marathon: My life has changed radically, and I would never go back for a second. The change the Lord has made has been lasting and real. Still, I have not been without sin these past couple of years. The Lord is chipping away at my pride and showing me that this really is going to be a long race with obstacles ahead; He is giving me the strength to run with endurance as I seek His face and draw close to Him. I'm humbled to have to share my weaknesses with you, but I continue to learn lessons through my mistakes.

There are two very clear lessons that I've learned in my failures over the last couple of years. But these are more than just lessons; they are warnings, and I would like to share them with you.

Warning #1: The Dangers of Victory

Purity is a wonderful thing, and walking in unmarred fellowship with Jesus Christ is the most wonderful thing I've experienced in my entire life, but when sinners like you or me walk in this strange and new state of being, our *pride* can get us into big trouble. We experience the victory, and somehow we think that it was something that we did, so we take credit for it.

This leads us into a vicious trap: When we think we did it ourselves, we think we are somehow immune to this sin all of a sudden! But the Bible warns, "So, if you think you are standing firm, be careful that you don't fall!" (1 Corinthians 10:12). Paul tells us that if we say that we are without sin, "we make [God] out to be a liar" (1 John 1:10). Christ died to give us victory over sin, and in the Bible He placed the instructions for how we might have this victory.

It is not enough only to follow these instructions, but it is also *imperative* that we give credit where credit is due. God warns us that "it is by grace that you have been saved, through faith—and this is not from yourselves, it is the gift of God—not by works, so that no one can boast" (Ephesians 2:8–9).

Thinking for one second that the victory we're having over this ensnaring sin is to our credit begins a slippery slope that will lead us right back to where we were in the first place. And, as Robert Daniels has warned in *The War Within,* "It is a long war, and there are numerous battles." We need to remember that our natural inclination is to sin. Our sin nature is ever with us. Without Christ leading our lives, we *will* sin.

Keeping Our Eyes on Jesus

I think back to the times when I fell again after I knew so much victory, and I can tell you that each time I did, my focus had shifted. My eyes were no longer trained on Jesus. It was much like Peter walking to Jesus on the water. Perhaps a young, single man in his sexual prime abstaining from sexual desires and sin and walking in purity day after day is as unnatural a thing as walking on water was for Peter!

Watch Peter carefully. Jesus called him out onto the water, which was a very unnatural thing for someone to ask, but Peter had enough faith in his Lord to go forward and do something he had never done, because it was Jesus calling him to do it. He fixed his eyes on Jesus, and he walked on the water! He did the very thing that most people might say was impossible. Yet when his gaze left Jesus and turned to the water, he began to sink. (See Matthew 14:24–31.)

So it was with me. When I fixed my eyes on Jesus Christ and became excited about sexual purity and pure, rich fellowship with Him, I walked in victory. But when I took my eyes off of my Lord, I forgot why I was fighting this fight. I forgot why I was running the race. My focus shifted off of Christ and how helpless I was without Him, and on to *my* victory and how good *I* was doing in overcoming sin. I lost my attitude of dependence on Christ and found out once again that I can't "walk on water" by myself.

Meanwhile, sin never lost its superficial and deceptive attraction, and I would think, *Why not?* I could give you dozens of reasons why not right now, but a sinner on his own doesn't listen to reason. It's a radical thing to walk with Christ, and it's a radical thing to be a pure single man.

We are commanded to "fix our eyes on Jesus, the author and perfecter of our faith" (Hebrews 12:2). What does it mean to fix our gaze on Jesus? The answer is a matter of the heart, of focus, time, and obedience. We have to wake up each morning hungry for Jesus. As I wrote in my journal all those days ago, we're never idle. We're either running after sin, or running after Christ and His righteousness. Those days when I would get lazy in my devotions, and I wouldn't truly gaze into the face of Christ—when I wouldn't take time to read the Bible carefully and hide God's Word in my heart—I would stumble. Eventually, if I didn't repent and fall back in the arms of Jesus, I would fall.

Warning #2: Beware of New Sins!

You *will* be tempted to new sexual sins. This warning is so imperative I must include it. It may be in other forms and with different struggles, but if you live long enough, I guarantee you will be presented with the same traps as I was, unless you heed these words now. I pray that you will.

There were always several sins that I struggled with. (Please understand that it doesn't matter if you struggle with the same particular sins as I—the application of the lesson is universal. Plug your own sins in for mine, and apply.) For me, it was always lust with my eyes and masturbation. I had never really struggled with pornography, or getting myself in tempting situations with girls. Sometimes this was due to the unavailability of either of these, but many other times they were available and I simply abstained. I prided myself on the false notion that I was immune to these sins. I didn't view pornography, and for the most part, I hadn't sinned physically with a girl.

Then, in the summer before my freshman year of college, I found myself in a whole new atmosphere. I was a lifeguard working and living at a major amusement park, and the temptation of lust was greater than I had ever known. For about two months, I lived with almost five thousand college-aged kids, and the sexual promiscuity was greater than I've ever seen. My friend who lived next door boasted that he slept with eight different girls one week. I lived in a small room with two other guys, and my roommates would have girls over to sleep with them in their beds. The majority of the guys at the amusement park were homosexual, so that greatly increased the odds for the straight guys to get girls.

I thought I was immune to these temptations. But the Scripture warns: "So, *if you think* you are standing firm, be careful that you don't fall!" (1 Corinthians 10:12, emphasis added). Soon my roommates moved out for the summer and I had the room to myself. I met a very pretty girl who was also a lifeguard, and I found out quickly that she was very interested in me. I got myself in a situation where the two of us were alone, and I turned my back on God and committed sins with her that I had never committed before. I had never done these things even before I was saved. By the grace of God and my fear of the consequences I didn't have sex with her, but what I did was as sinful in God's eyes as sex. The point is, I sinned.

I fell into the fallacy of moral relativism. I thought that since people around me were being so downright immoral—committing fornication and having homosexual sex regularly, then making out with a girl and doing other things short of sex would not be that bad. Also, I was lonely, and I was bored. God gave me plenty of chances to get out (1 Corinthians 10:13), but I rejected them. I chose sin instead of Christ that day, even though I had never fallen into that sort of sin before.

Similarly, when I fell into the sin of Internet pornography for the first time in college (see chapter 8), I thought I was immune. I didn't even go to the required meeting where they showed the freshman guys a video warning about the effects of pornography. I put myself in a tempting situation and had not built up any defenses against it, and I fell into a brand-new sin for the first time at eighteen years old. The Scripture is true: "If you think you are standing firm, be careful that you don't fall!"

The Lesson

The lesson I learned from those two heartbreaking experiences is that *I am not immune to any sin!* Just because I have not fallen into a particular sinful practice before, it does not mean that I wouldn't be capable of falling into that sin if I found myself in the wrong situation at the wrong time. In other words, there's a first time for everything!

So what are we to do about this? *Beware—stay away—* and *run!* Just believing and knowing that we are capable of all sorts of evil, even those we have not previously dealt with, is a giant first step.

Grateful for the Lessons

I praise God with all my heart that I've learned all this at such a relatively early age. I've been up to my neck in sin, and there have been various consequences, but by the abundant and generous grace of God I can still look forward to a wonderful future in Him. There are some lessons God would teach each of us: Be faithful in the small things; only then can we become faithful in the big things. Also, you and I are susceptible to sin, and we must be wary of feeling we are immune.

I'm in my early twenties and single. I have the opportunity to embrace these lessons now and therefore save myself years of heartache in the future. As we heed these warnings we can protect ourselves for our future career, ministry, marriage, and family. Decide to stay out of suggestive and tempting situations as much as possible, and if ever you must be in some setting that could turn tempting, then *fix your eyes on Jesus Christ* and keep your commitments to Him and your family.

Praise God for this wonderful lesson now, rather than later, whatever the cost! Dear brother, please learn this lesson, right now, along with me. God only wants His best for us. Let us heed His warnings and His promises, today and the rest of our lives.

REFLECTIONS

1. *Have you ever fallen into a trap of committing some sin for the first time because you thought you were immune to it? How did it happen?*

2. *What are some things that you have never struggled with? How will you practically guard against these things, so that you never do fall into them?*

3. *Take some time to praise the Lord for all that He's forgiven you for, and for all the bad things that He rescued you from because He saved you when He did.*

> **❝** To take a girl's virginity is to take a part of her. . . . You cannot take a girl's virginity without creating emotional scars in her that may last for years or perhaps a lifetime if she doesn't find God's healing and hope. For one brief moment, stop thinking with your sex drive and think of her future.
>
> **BOB GRESH**
> *Who Moved the Goalpost?*

Treat younger men as brothers, older women as mothers, and ***younger women as sisters, with absolute purity.***

1 Timothy 5:1–2 (emphasis added)

CHAPTER 13

"Dear Brother," from Your Sister in Christ

W E guys get so hung up on the morality and obligation of sexual purity that we often forget that there is a *human* side to our lust, as well as other sexual sins. This sin is not just against ourselves and, more important, against God—it is against all the girls who are the objects of our lust and the victims of our sin.

To get a better perspective of how our sin affects the women we sin against, I went right to the source: the women themselves. I sent out interview letters to a number of Christian women, and I was overwhelmed by the responses. After reading their comments, I want even more to live a life of absolute purity and to be nothing but a blessing in the lives of my sisters. I think you will feel the same way, so I'm going to give you a chance to read their comments the same way I did—without any input from me. I'll just throw some questions out there and let the ladies do all the talking. It's their turn to be heard.

What Is Lust?

"Lust is a violation of my personhood. I am more than a prize to be won, a product to be used, or anyone's property to be bought. Lust ignores my worth as an intelligent individual and reduces me to an object of desire."

"Lust is a gross perversion of what is intended to be good."

"At the heart of it, lust is ultimately selfishness. It's taking someone else and thinking not of their good or what they need, but using them for a selfish purpose. It reduces the object of it to simply that—an object. The person who is being lusted after is no longer a human being, but rather an item to satisfy another person's longings. Lust is the opposite of love—it is selfish and uses others for one's sinful passions."

What Is It Like to Be a Girl in This Carnal World?

"Being a girl in this carnal world is not easy. We're surrounded by media that depict women as sexual objects, and our femininity is

often either condemned by feminists or sexualized to the extent that it's awkward to look at ourselves as beautiful creations of God.

"It's degrading to be considered nothing more than a body for male sexual gratification, and it's demoralizing to look around and recognize that many women exist who buy into the stereotype, and so validate the assumption that women are to be regarded as simply sexual beings.

"It's also scary to think that I may be giving myself to a man in marriage someday, and he is surrounded by such a moral laxity that he will struggle to be faithful to me. Jesus said that looking at a woman lustfully is the same as adultery; yet in today's society, it seems acceptable to look as long as you don't touch (even among Christian men). To know that the men who surround me at college are technically guilty of 'adultery' against their future wives is so discouraging. It's difficult to trust when we look around and see so many men—even Christian men—even Christian leaders—engaged in such sexual sin. It's obvious that the context can't change; our society is our society, and it has been this way since time began. So something within the man must change."

"It is very difficult. Every day we are bombarded with implicit and explicit messages of what we are to look like, how we are to act, etc. Most girls feel they need to be size 0 with the perfect hair, perfect skin . . . the perfect 'image.' We have learned of the power we possess, and we use it very well . . . but in the wrong ways. We flaunt our outward beauty because that is what we are told is most important.

"To be honest, I don't believe I know one girl who is completely satisfied with how God created her. I, myself, struggle with my image more often than I'd like to admit, and why do I do that? I shouldn't because I know the creator of this universe finds me most beautiful, and yet I put down His creation so often."

"It is hard because girls want to know that they are beautiful and they will sometimes do anything for attention, even if it is negative attention. It is easy to get negative attention. The girls that go for negative attention get what they want and the rest have to wait patiently. That's hard to do."

"Dude, it's not easy. Guys are often oblivious to the safety concerns that women face every day. For instance, my brother went to Europe to study at Oxford University and spent nearly every weekend traveling, often by himself. I would love such an experience, but it simply is not available to me. A young girl cannot travel around Europe by herself or even accompanied by one other girl or guy. It just doesn't work. It's hard to be independent."

"It is so hard not to buy into the lie that relationships are all about sex, and girls need to be beautiful to 'catch' as many guys as possible, and that girls need to work to get guys. This is all not true; they are lies that the world tries to sell us. It's hard not to accept them, because, quite frankly, sometimes it seems like the world is right. Guys do flock to the girls who dress badly, or even just to the girls who flirt and try to get guys' attention (even if they dress modestly). Relationships are very physical, and we all have longings and desires for physical intimacy. It's hard not to think that the world's right when you get ignored by guys. It's depressing, quite frankly. It's really hard to try to be pure and do what is right. There is tremendous pressure to be otherwise. Only with the support of friends (guys especially), can we do it.

"Honestly, I don't know what I would do without my brother. He has been my support this year—constantly challenging me not to drop my standards but to keep them high, to keep myself above the 'tricks' that girls play to attract guys. He's done this by telling me I'm worth something for being me, for my mind, for my soul, and for everything else God gave me—not just my

body or any relationships I have. This is the thing that keeps me going."

How Does It Make You Feel When a Guy Looks at You Lustfully?

"Dirty . . . like a piece of my purity is being taken away. It makes me wonder if I'm doing something wrong and I want to crawl into a little hole and never let guys see me again.

"It makes me feel cheap and dirty. I feel like they have stolen something from me that was only mine to give."

"This has changed from high school to college. In high school, I enjoyed being looked at by guys. Because it was then and only then that I felt beautiful, even though I 'know' the guy was just being perverted. It made me feel good temporarily, and those temporary feelings are what led me to long for feelings/satisfaction outside of Jesus, which caused Him and me great pain.

"Now that I've matured, I actually cringe, with anger and hurt, when a guy looks at me lustfully. Because now I truly 'know' he is not thinking wholesome thoughts and is only thinking of me as an object. One side of me wants to smack him, the other wants me to cry for him, because I know how much he is missing out on, which is the beautiful plan God has intricately created for him to fulfill."

"It makes me feel angry. It is so demeaning to women when men look at them lustfully."

"I feel degraded. I feel like my only worth is because of my body. I hate it when the only guys that invite me to spend time with them are the ones that have some interest in me beyond friendship."

"On the one hand, to be looked up and down by a guy, or 'checked out' by a man, seems pleasant at first. It makes a girl feel like she has power—like she has something that a guy wants—like she's worth something.

"This feeling, however, doesn't erase the feeling of disgust and shame that accompany being lusted after. We know that's not what we were created for, and that lust is not the kind of attention we long for. We long to be treasured for who we are—not what we look like. The problem is that we rarely get attention for that from the world. We get attention for our bodies. So, we dress in ways that hurt men and make them struggle, and we get the attention we crave. Yet, it's not the kind of attention we really desire. But it's all we get, so we lie to ourselves and accept it. We tell ourselves that we just need to get used to it.

"The more time I spend with my Christian brothers, who treat me as a sister—someone to be treasured and loved simply because I'm God's—the easier it is for me to have the right perspective. The respect of my brothers-in-Christ is so much more important to me than the attention of men. When I feel loved and cared for by my brothers-in-Christ, I feel disgusted by lust. It has no appeal to me."

What Do You Wish Guys Knew About Girls?

"Girls truly admire and long for LEADERS. I don't think guys re-alize how much girls want to have a man that is truly passionate for the Lord, who will challenge them spiritually, and will be a leader for God and for the household. We girls look around and see flirty, immature guys, and how often we settle for them be-cause we think we'll never meet the 'Prince Charming' we long for. So, guys, please stand up, put your eyes on the prize, and fol-low after Christ. We girls are watching and waiting and wanting!

"I do wish guys would be more careful with our hearts. Yes, we girls are responsible with when we give our hearts away, but it is SO easy for us to be swooned. Please don't touch or talk in such a way that may cause even the slightest hint of interest unless you truly are interested in pursuing something. And if you are interested, be open and honest—do not make it a game of guessing and flirting."

"Christian girls generally are not impressed by guys who are boastful, shallow, or apathetic, but by men of humility, leader-ship, and a heart that seeks the things of God."

"I wish guys knew how fragile we girls are on the inside. If guys knew how fragile and sensitive most girls really are, they wouldn't try to take advantage of girls the way they do. I think they would be much gentler. I don't want to characterize all guys as being rough and only trying to take advantage of girls. Many aren't; but the ones who are disrespectful and demeaning towards girls hurt girls much more than they realize.

"I think many girls look for security and stability in a re-lationship with a guy and also want to look to someone for leader-ship. Thinking or knowing that that guy has ulterior motives or other interests at heart rather than being motivated by sincere love is very hurtful."

"I would tell guys that they send conflicting messages when they say that they want to be a 'good Christian brother' or even just a 'good friend' to every girl but then only talk to, invite, and hang out with the obviously gorgeous ones. It hurts, and it's not a good testimony. There is certainly nothing wrong with being closer to one girl or having a group of core girl friends as long as they're treating all girls with equal courtesy, as a true brother should."

"I wish Christian guys knew that girls desperately need affirmation and assurance. We need to feel loved and cared for. We are relational people, and relationships with just girls do not fulfill us totally. We need affirmation from guys as well. We need to feel protected, cared for, and treasured. A good deal of this should come from our fathers and brothers, granted. However, if we are the children of God, then we are brothers and sisters. Some of that responsibility falls on Christian guys. Just as Christian girls are charged with being sisters to Christian guys, and protecting their eyes, Christian guys must be willing to accept the responsibility to protect their sisters' hearts.

"Even if we act as if we are tough and don't need love, we do. Believe me, I've been there. I act as if I don't need any-one, or can handle things on my own. That is completely un-true. I need friends. More than that, I need brothers in Christ. Girls need guys to affirm them and show them that they are worth something. A lot of times, girls act the way that they do because they don't get affirmation from men. We aren't loved by

our brothers in Christ. . . . We turn to dressing immodestly and behaving shamefully because we want affirmation from men!

"Instead, if Christian guys were to actually treat their Christian sisters as sisters instead of possibilities, things might be very different. What exactly do I mean?!? Well, think of how a brother treats his sister—he loves her for who she is—her personality, her character, her sense of humor, her gifts, her weaknesses—not her body. He does things for her. He tells her that she's special because God made her that way. He treats her like a woman. He takes care of her gently when she's weak. He encourages her to pursue her passions and dreams. He loves her—can hug her—without lusting after her. This is what we need in our Christian brothers!"

"Dear Brother," from Your Sister in Christ

You may never really know what is in a person's heart when you talk with them. And guys, we may never know how badly what we do may wound the girl we're lusting after or taking advantage of. The next three letters are from three dear friends of mine. They are three of the sweetest, nicest girls you ever want to meet. These aren't angry, in-your-face girls who go around saying things like this to people. They're wonderful Christian girls who go through life hiding all of the pain, guilt, and regret inside of them caused by guys they trusted. All I did was ask them to share what they would say to the guys who hurt them if they got the chance, and this is what they wrote. (All names shown have been changed to protect the individuals.)

Dear Ben,

    I wanted to write and tell you how horrible you made me feel this past summer. Although you may have not known that I knew about your comments, I did and they disgusted me. I have never had anyone make me feel so used in all my life. Your comments were not only inappropriate but degrading and demeaning. You first of all have no right to even think those thoughts about me or verbalize them. I felt ashamed to be a woman and that made me mad. I was so angry at you that I didn't know how to express myself. Although I have forgiven you, know I want to know that it was one of the worst experiences I ever had to go through and I wish you could know how it felt. Don't take things that are not yours.

                        —Kate

John,

    Please don't ever hurt me again. You do it so well, by telling me you want it to be over, and then you call me. Why do you do that? When we say it is over I deal with that, then you call me wanting more? We cannot be friends, not with our past. Also, please don't cheat on me, or force me to have sex with you, or be controlling of my life. I hate you now, and I probably always will, even though I pray about it. You did a good job of making me hate you, so I have come to the conclusion that that is how you wanted it all along. Well done—you have succeeded.

                        —Beth

Dear Bill,

I am so angry and hurt right now. How fooled I was! I
thought I had finally met a quality guy, one who would respect
me and my beliefs and standards. You said you would; in fact,
you said you totally agreed with my beliefs and standards, and
that it made you that much more excited to be with me. Why
did I listen? Because I longed to be with someone who would
respect me and my God (our God actually, since you are a believer).

I thought our relationship was going to be different. You
were the only guy I ever asked permission from my father to
date, because I knew we were going to be different. The third
day after my dad said yes to us, you took advantage of me
and touched me in the most disrespectful way!!! I was so
scared . . . so shocked . . . I didn't even know how to respond.
After you left that night, I cried myself to sleep . . . because I
once again had fooled myself into thinking this relationship
would be different. I never did bring it up because I was so
embarrassed. I didn't want you to look down on me and then
spread rumors at school. So I kept it to myself, even though I
was so angry and hurt.

Why would you tell me one thing and do another? You
didn't really respect me. You didn't really respect my beliefs.
You didn't even care about my standards. Shoot, you didn't
even care about God. You're a liar, a user, and a heartbreaker.

It took me a year and a half to forgive you, and when I
did, you made me sound so dumb and pathetic. Well, excuse
me for being so hurt over what you did to me.

As I look back on our situation, our relationship . . . I do
realize now that we should never have dated because I knew I
wasn't strong, and what would it have hurt to wait? So often
I find myself wanting things right here, right now, when it

would be so much better to wait. That's what we should have done . . . waited. Then we would never have dated, never have fought, never have to "break up," never have to ignore each other for over a year after that break up.

So we both did things that were wrong . . . but for your sake, learn to respect a girl! Not only does her heart need to be protected but so does her body. Her body belongs to one person, and that one person is her husband. Help hold her accountable to that.

—Lisa

REFLECTIONS

1. *What are your reactions to these comments? How did they make you feel by reading them?*

2. *What stuck out to you the most about what the girls said? What patterns or recurring themes did you notice in their comments?*

3. *What changes or decisions do you need to make in your life, knowing how your sin affects the girls around you?*

❝ Whether your hurts are deep or relatively mild, it is wise to be honest about them in the context of affirming relationships so that healing can begin.

ROBERT MCGEE
The Search for Significance

For we do not have a high priest who is unable to sympathize with our weaknesses, but we have one who has been tempted in every way, just as we are—yet was without sin. Let us then approach the throne of grace with confidence, so that we may receive mercy and find grace to help us in our time of need.

Hebrews 4:15–16

CHAPTER 14

A Deeper Pain

WE'VE come a long way together in our battle for purity, but we're not quite finished. We need to wrestle through three other issues—deeper issues in our hearts we need to deal with for true healing to take place, other struggles we have not yet covered, and other dangers of sexual sin that we may not have considered. Of the three topics discussed in the next three sections, most guys will relate to the first one and some to the second. But be sure to read about the third issue, for the final section is critical for every single guy to consider.

What's Really Going On in That Heart of Yours?

So far, we've faced a lot of different reasons that we stumble and fall sexually, and we've looked at numerous strategies for fighting back and winning battles against the enemy who's been waging war on us for so long. These things are all important, and they can do astonishing things in our lives if we put them into practice. However, there may be pain or resentment in our hearts, and unless we deal with these deeper issues, we will never be fully healed, and any victory we gain over sexual sin will only be temporary. The most common deeper issue we face is rejection and loneliness.

There is an emptiness inside of us that grows each time we're rejected or hurt by someone we trusted and loved. I've never felt more vulnerable than when I've been rejected—whether by girls, or friends, or family. I've spoken with dozens of guys, and I have yet to find one who doesn't agree that pornography, masturbation, and even fornication can all be forms of escape from the pain that's embedded in our hearts. Robert Daniels understood this when he wrote in *The War Within*, "For many men sexual orgasm provides an escape from pain and the hurts of the past." Many guys even say that loneliness is a greater contributor to their struggle than lust. What can we do about this?

One major remedy is strong, God-honoring relationships. God made us to be in relationship with Him and others. First Corinthians 12:12–30 tells us that we need each other spiritually, and the same is true emotionally. I'm talking about building strong, meaningful friendships with both guys and girls who will love you, affirm you, listen to you, and laugh with you. During a Bible conference entitled "My Times Are in Your Hands," Alistair Begg taught us that "if you have just one friend in this life whom you can share your heart with and who will not trample it all over town, you are rich."

The more time I spend and the more I laugh with my dearest friends, the less prone I am to sexual temptation, and the easier it is to be content in my singleness. It is important that our closest friends are guys, but forging platonic friendships with girls can enrich our lives as well. Rebecca St. James agrees. She writes in her book *Wait for Me*, "Do you want to know how to not be so lonely while you're waiting for 'the one'? Invest in relationships with friends of the opposite sex. Not only will this help you realize that you're not facing the world alone, but you will also learn from those relationships."[1] But when you do, just remember that girls can stumble emotionally as much as we can sexually; we should never become emotionally intimate with any woman other than our wife.

And how do we make these friends? I'll risk the cliché to make the point: The best way to make friends is to be a friend. Give your life away and you will be amazed at how others will want to invest time in you (see John 12:25; 15:13).

What About My Struggle?

There are also people who are struggling with a variety of things that haven't been tackled here. I haven't forgotten you. While the things we've dealt with have been the most common issues that we single guys deal with in the area of sexuality, I realize they aren't the only issues. I will not insult you by trying to tackle all of these things that are outside the scope of this book. Instead, I would like to point you in the direction of other resources that can help you.

If you're struggling with other areas of sexuality, such as adultery, homosexuality, or incest, or if you've made poor decisions that have hurt others emotionally or physically, then please read the book *The War Within*, by Robert Daniels. For additional resources on issues such as homosexuality, depression, and sexual addiction, see my Web site, www.josephknable.com, for more information.

If you know that your sexual struggle is an escape from some deeper issue like depression, rejection, or abandonment, I recommend *The Search for Significance,* by Robert S. McGee. If you have some emotional or personal issue that needs immediate attention, see a counselor. I recommend Rapha, a highly reputable Christian counseling center. Call Rapha toll-free, twenty-four hours a day, at 1-800-227-2657. Confidentiality is guaranteed.

Let's Not Be Causers of Pain

The letter and challenge of this section comprise perhaps the most important section in this book, so please read them carefully and prayerfully. We learned in chapter 13 that it's not just ourselves whom we can hurt when we sin. Read the following letter that a dear friend wrote to a man who wounded her worse than anyone else ever has. We'll call her Anne. While the names have been changed to protect those involved, and the letter has never been delivered, everything you read is real. This is Anne's story.

Dear James,

After my parents got divorced, my mom met you and you moved into my house. There were so many changes going on at the time. I tried to make you feel welcome. It was difficult. My mom was supposed to be with dad, not you! I wanted Mom to be happy so I accepted it and let you in my life. I thought maybe, just maybe, this would mean I would finally have more stability. I soon found out just how wrong I was.

I can't really remember how all of it started. I have tried to block out a lot of what happened while you were living with us. I noticed you had started drinking heavier and would often come home drunk. I didn't know how to respond.

Things just changed. You started treating my mom differently, and would call her all kinds of names. When I heard this I would just sit in my room and cry. I knew it was not right for you to treat my mom that way, but what could I do? I was only a little girl and Mom said she needed you.

My mom ended up having to switch to a night shift at work. One night when I was feeling sick I saw you lying on the couch so I told you I didn't feel well. You said I could lie with you until Mom came home, and that you would take care of me. I thought you were being nice, but then when I had fallen asleep you started to touch me in places I knew were not right. I felt so uncomfortable but I didn't know what to do, so I just froze. So many thoughts went through my head, but I just lay there until you were finished and you made sure I went back to bed so Mom wouldn't know anything, and you told me not to tell her.

I had so many thoughts and feelings rush through me. I had many questions but, most of all I was afraid and ashamed. The next morning when I had to wake up and face you, I couldn't even look at you the same. But I didn't want anyone to know, especially my mom. So I had to go on as if nothing happened. I learned to put a smile on the outside but on the inside I was damaged. I remember coming off the school bus and having to walk through the living room to my bedroom while you were watching pornographic movies and doing what you did to satisfy your sexual desires. Your drinking became even more constant, and I know now that you were sleeping around with other women besides my mom. I didn't feel comfortable in my own home so I tried to go to friends' houses whenever possible. I loved to go to school because there I did not have to worry about anything. I felt safe.

I have obviously grown up now, but what you did has not diminished. I have faced many tear-filled nights, but I am thankful that the Lord is faithful and He has healed my wounds. I have recognized that what you did against me He hated and that it was sin. I do not blame myself or my God for what happened. I have forgiven you because I see how Christ has forgiven me for my sins.

How could this have happened? What made you do such a thing to a helpless 11-year-old child?

I have concluded that you allowed sin to creep into your life and take over. Somehow women had become objects to you. I pray that God will help you and other men to see women as they truly are and not as objects to be lusted over.

I am so grateful that God has helped me to forgive you, James, and has blessed me with a wonderful man who is now my fiancé and will soon be my husband. He respects me as a woman and has helped me to see there are men that care about women and want what is best for them.

—Anne

I know that wasn't any fun to read. It also wasn't any fun to sit and listen as Anne told me the story in the first place, and then to read the letter for the first time when she sent it to me, but I've shared it with you for a purpose. Anne is my friend, and reading what her mom's boyfriend did to her infuriates me to the core. I can't stand it. I am so grateful for what a beautiful, confident woman God has made her, but I know that for every one like her, who was able to forgive and have a productive, joyful life, there are many others who are forever scarred and can never see themselves as a worthy daughter of God, let alone trust any other man.

You may think you would never molest a girl or rape a woman. Yet each of us has the capacity to hurt a woman emotionally or physically. That's why we must not ignore the wounds of the past or bad patterns of the present.

When it comes to women, there are two kinds of men in this world. First, there are those who steal and rob from women; men who abuse them and hurt them emotionally, physically, and sexually. This can be as small as persisting to go further with your girlfriend when she's told you to stop or playing games with her emotions in a relationship, or as big as raping a woman or molesting a child. This is the kind of guy that makes many women embittered toward men, and rightly so—the kind of guy who makes some women unable to trust a man in any relationship, and causes other women to cry themselves to sleep most nights.

Then there is the other kind of man—the kind that gives women hope that perhaps not all men are rotten. The kind that they trust to protect them from the first kind. This man is gentle, loving, and understanding. This is the kind of guy that Anne finally found, and has pledged her hand to in marriage.

Our Potential to Help or Hurt

You know what the kicker is? You and I have the potential to be either one. We have the potential to hurt girls or to help them. We could be the guy who scars a woman so badly that she never recovers, or we can be the guy who helps her in the process of restoration. You might think I'm crazy, but I don't think that James ever thought that he would grow up to be a guy sitting on a couch watching porn and molesting an eleven-year-old girl in her own house. If we're careless and allow the sinful habits we've developed to grow, there's no telling where it will stop. One survey of nearly six thousand teenagers described as "religious" found that almost one-third of females in the eleventh and twelfth grades reported an unwanted sexual experience. I don't even want to know how high the percentage would be among twenty-five- or thirty-year-old women.[2]

Make a decision right now about which guy you're going to be. Whether or not you've already developed destructive habits that could lead to something worse, go back and apply the things you've learned here, and do whatever it takes to set your life on the course of purity, by the power of the living God. I'm determined that I shall be the kind of guy that a girl wants to run to, not from. Strengthen your resolve today. Let's not be causers of pain.

REFLECTIONS

1. *Is there any deeper pain that you need to deal with? Whatever it is, please share it with a pastor or mentor today, and determine together how you're going to try to tackle those issues, with the suggestions listed in mind.*

2. *Which of the two types of guys are you going to be? How?*

❝❝ I have either got to overcome the world, or the world is going to overcome me. I have either got to conquer sin in me—or sin about me—and get it under my feet, or it is going to conquer me . . . We have this to encourage us: we are assured of victory at the end. We are promised a glorious triumph.

D. L. MOODY
Moody's Stories

To him who is able to keep you from falling and to present you before his glorious presence without fault and with great joy—to the only God our Savior be glory, majesty, power and authority, through Jesus Christ our Lord, before all ages, now and forevermore!

Jude 24–25

CHAPTER 15

What Life Do You Want?

DEAR BROTHER, thank you for sticking with me through this journey. I don't assume it has been easy for you to wrestle with these issues, and at times you may have wished you had never picked up this book. It has not been easy for me to share all of these things with you, either. But it has been good, and I pray that we would both grow closer to our Lord Jesus Christ because of it.

As you set the book down to continue through life's difficult journey, with all the temptations that our sinful natures, our carnal culture, and our enemy the devil will throw at us, may you remember two key words when it comes to this battle for purity: *run* and *grace*.

We will never be immune from the temptations that

will come our way, so we must always do like Joseph did and *run* from any temptation that comes our way. We must run from sin and run after Christ. I can guarantee that you and I will always be running in one direction or the other. It's up to us which direction we head.

At all times, let us remember that we are governed by *grace,* and that Jesus Christ's *grace* will have the final word in the defense of our lives before God. There are a thousand reasons and a thousand rewards to living a pure and holy life—I'll include my favorite three in this chapter, but let us be primarily motivated by *grace,* and let the *grace* of God fill our hearts with joy and peace. Oh, how I praise God for all He's done and all that He's continuing to do!

Our Filthy, Burning House

As you begin to gain victory in your struggle with sexual sin, you will notice that some unusual things will happen. Many will be encouraging and exciting, but some will be challenging and even disheartening. The disheartenment comes when we realize how much sin is left in our lives, *other* than sexual sin! I'll explain what I mean.

Think of your life as a house. This house is cluttered and filthy with trash and dirt all over it, but it's also on fire. Sure, you'd like to clean it up, but you're never able to do any cleaning because you have to spend all your energy trying to keep the fire from getting out of control! There's nothing you can do or even care to do about all that clutter and mess while the thing is in danger of burning to the ground. In fact, you probably don't even realize how dirty your house has become since the fire started. But once you do put out the fire, you look around and see the mess that's left.

There's a pile of pride over there, and in the closet you find a mountain of selfish ambition. There's some rudeness cluttering up the counters, and there is so much jealousy and unforgiveness piled under the beds that it can be seen from all sides. The fire is out, but there is still so much work to be done. This can be a very discouraging time.

We each have a choice as to how the story will go in our lives. Many guys spend their whole lives fighting the fire of their sexual transgressions, so that they are never able to work on cleaning up everything else that's wrong with their lives. This means they will always have several things that annoy others or hurt others that they may never become aware of. Other men let the fires burn their house down—their lives are ruined by their sexual exploits. Still others put out the fire, and when they see the mess that remains, they give up and become apathetic, and before they know it they're fighting the fire again.

But there are some guys—a few good men of God—who put out that fire, see the mess that remains, and *they go to work*. They humbly accept what the Lord has revealed to them and they thank Him for helping them to change.

The Lord has helped me to put out the fire for the most part in my life (although the pilot light of my lust will always be lit and can flame up at any moment if ignored or encouraged). When He did He showed me that there were many other areas that need a lot of work. This was not easy, and I was very humbled to find that out. But I'm glad that I did, and I praise my sweet Lord Jesus for caring so much about me to want me to change. This is the very thesis of Max Lucado's book *Just Like Jesus:* "Jesus loves you just the way you are, but He refuses to leave you that way. He wants you to be *Just Like Jesus.*"

Brother, are you willing for Jesus to work in your life like this? Are you willing to find out that there is much in your life that needs to change? I hope that you are. If so, brace yourself, but brace yourself on the grace and love and forgiveness of Jesus Christ, and look forward to becoming more like Him than you ever thought possible.

Three Dreams

I'm a huge dreamer, and I hope you are too. I firmly believe that the Lord wants us to dream big, but He wants us to submit our dreams to Him and to allow for Him to change our dreams as He shows us His will for our lives. There are three big dreams I have that will be realized as I run from sin and allow Christ to conform me to His likeness.

Dream #1: Greater Fellowship

The first dream that will come true when we start living in victory is the improved state of fellowship we have with our God and our loved ones. The more I get to know the Lord Jesus and all that He is to me, the more I can agree with Paul when he said, "I consider everything a loss compared to the surpassing greatness of knowing Christ Jesus my Lord" (Philippians 3:8). Nothing has separated me more from the fellowship of Christ than my selfish sexual sin, and nothing has made it sweeter than when I have thrown this sin off and walked in purity.

This sweetened fellowship also includes the relationships we have with other people. When I'm not so discouraged and ashamed with myself because of the sexual sin I'm entangled in, my relationships with my friends and family are so much richer and more wholesome. This is especially true with women. My relationships with my female friends are deepened because I am seeing them as people and not objects.

An invaluable, untapped treasure exists for Christian men: genuine friendships with other women of God. But we'll never be able to enjoy that treasure if our heads are full of garbage and our minds are in the gutter.

I've begun to see what I've been missing out on, and I thank God for the awesome gift of friendships with my sisters in Christ. Don't miss out, brother!

Dream #2: Closer Family

No other dream has claimed more of my heart and thoughts over the course of my life than my persistent and gigantic dream of being a godly husband and father. Nothing in this life excites me more than the thought of becoming best friends and falling in love with one of God's most precious daughters, marrying her, and sharing all of my remaining days on earth with her. My heart skips at the thought of having a son and daughter whom I could call my own—and then to partner with my wife in raising them in the love of Christ and the instruction of His Word.

I once read, "The difference between a dream and a goal is a plan." My dream for family is also a goal, because I do have a plan. That plan includes living my single life in purity and holiness. In our world and society, there is no way we can have one without the other.

More than half of all Christians get a divorce. There are a number of reasons why this happens, but we must ask ourselves why we should be any different. If we're being careless with our sexual lives now, sleeping with women who aren't our wives and consuming pornography, we're setting ourselves up to fall into these same practices when we're married! I've heard over and over again that people do not get any better once you marry them. That's a scary thought for a young lady! Granted, God can do any work at any time, but the *trend* is that those who make provision for failure will be given to it later in life. I intend to *never* cheat on my wife, whether by another woman or by pornography, but I won't do it by sheer willpower or just stubbornly thinking I'm beyond those things. I'll do it by the power of God because I'm making every provision for holiness *today,* and I will continue to do this throughout my life.

What about you? What makes you think that you won't be among the *majority* of Christians whose marriages end up in divorce? If you share this dream with me, brother, then join me in developing a plan to attain it. Of course, I do not know if the Lord has any of these blessings in store for me; He may keep me single for His good purpose. It's clear that Paul, himself unmarried all his days, saw being single a good state, and indeed a gift that God has given some men and women. (See 1 Corinthians 7:7–9, 25–38.)

There's debate over what Paul was driving at in 1 Corinthians 7, but one major implication is clear: A life of singleness is a high calling from God that can allow a person to serve Him with an undivided heart and schedule, and God *is* calling some of us to such a service. I think that the singleness calling is given greater emphasis because *perhaps the ones who are to remain single will need more encouragement and admonishment than the ones who are to be married.*

I have two married siblings and heaps of married friends, and most of them did not need much encouragement to make that decision—they were glad to! But many of my single friends and I struggle with our current single calling from time to time. I am very grateful to Paul for the encouragement that *we singles are not just killing time until either marriage or death.* No! *We're living a great adventure and heeding a high calling today, for which our Lord Jesus is quite pleased.*

I have found that believing in and embracing this calling from God, along with pouring myself into something the Lord has given me a clear passion and calling toward, are two things that can make my single calling exciting, fulfilling, and invigorating.

That being said, I still do hope for the privilege of being a husband and father someday. It's OK to honestly and candidly express your desires to the Lord—just be prepared for Him to answer your prayers in a way you didn't expect.

I wrote these three letters for my future family, if God has that particular blessing in store for me. I want to share them with you, brother.

To My Future Wife

Hi. My precious angel, I love you even though I don't know who you are. I've loved you for a very long time, and there is a GREAT BIG place in my heart that is reserved especially for you. I pray for you almost every day, and I have for years and years. I often wonder where you are and what you're doing as I go through this season of life without you. I'm looking forward so much to sharing all the days that the Lord will give us together. Unless the Lord should rapture us both home first, I hope we are able to spend many years together and grow very old caught in each other's loving gaze.

Sweetheart, I look forward to falling in love with you and starting my life with you more than anything else on earth, but I would be wrong to say that I can't wait. I can wait, by the grace of God and the blessing of His fellowship. He is my rock and my fortress, and I'll never expect you to meet the needs in my life that only He can fill. It's because I love Him and I love you so much that I will wait. I have much growing to do before our Father would entrust me with His most precious daughter. I am determined to be the very best husband possible, and I'm delighted to tell you that

God is daily breaking me and humbling me and molding me to become that husband who is worthy of your love. I'll wait for you, and I'll save myself for you. I'm not going to give any other woman anything that belongs to you: of my body or my heart.

For the mistakes I've made and will make, I'm sorry, and I beg your forgiveness. But I make no excuses for sin and I make every provision not to sin; by God's grace and power I will be faithful to you. Thank you for your faithfulness to me.

I absolutely know already that you're more precious than I could ever deserve, and I can only thank my God for you. I know you'll be far from perfect, but our gracious Lord will allow me to see you that way, and the rest of the time I'll choose to think that way. I plan on loving you just the way that Christ loved the church: sacrificially, unconditionally, and completely. I'm going to let you be who you are and I'm not going to stop you from becoming the woman that God is making you.

I love you so much, and I look forward with all of my heart to meeting you. Until then, God keep you in the name of our Lord and Savior, Jesus Christ, and forevermore afterward.

To My Future Daughters

God bless you, my little princess. I love you so dearly, even though the Lord has not even made you yet! But He already knows your name, He knows what color your hair is, He knows the outfit you're going to wear on your first day of kindergarten. I want to do everything in the world that I can to protect you and to show you the love of your heavenly Father. I pray for you even now as well, sweetie. I pray that you would come to trust the Lord Jesus at an early age, and you would know the joy of following and knowing Him.

I want you to be completely proud of your daddy, so I'm letting the Lord work in my life now so that I can be the very best daddy I can be. I look forward to taking you on sleigh rides, to reading you stories as you curl up next to me on the couch, to watching you play your violin or whatever it is you choose to do.

There are some things I need to warn you about, sweetheart. Don't ever let a boy take advantage of you, and be ever so very careful with your heart. Be careful with the hearts of boys as well, and look out for them in the way that you dress and behave around them.

I'm so happy that God will allow me to be your daddy, and I thank God for all the fun times we'll have. May God bless you and keep you and guide you and protect you all the days of your life, in the name of Jesus Christ our Lord and Savior.

To My Future Sons

God bless you, my son. I pray for you along with your mom and sisters, even though you're still waiting to be born! (Gee, that wait must be boring.) I've spent my whole life watching other dads to learn how I should love you and raise you. I've spent the most time watching our Father in heaven. I hope to be as much like Him to you as possible.

You have much to learn, my dear son. Oh, but there is so much to look forward to! There's sports, and flying, and arts, and food; oh, the food! There are places to see and so many cool people to meet (including girls! But don't be in a hurry; there's plenty of time for that). But let me tell you right off the bat the most important thing you'll ever learn: that Jesus Christ came to save you from your sins and that following Him is the most fulfilling and exciting thing you could ever do in your life. I pray that you would put your trust in the Lord much earlier than I did, so that you can start enjoying Him that much sooner.

I need to warn you about some things, little buddy. This is a pretty awful world to live in if you want to be holy and follow the Lord. You're going to have to trust the Lord and take heed of all of His instruction so that you won't be ripped to shreds by its evil and carnality. (We'll talk more about that when you get here and, you know, learn to talk.) But trust in the Lord and you will do amazing things for the kingdom of God. I pray that you would do even greater things than I do.

I commit you now to God, in the name of my Lord and Savior, Jesus Christ, for all the days of your life.

Dream #3: The Hope of Heaven

The psalmist yearned to be in the presence of God:

> *How lovely is your dwelling place, O LORD Almighty!*
> *My soul yearns, even faints, for the courts of the*
> *LORD; my heart and my flesh cry out for the living*
> *God. . . . Better is one day in your courts*
> *than a thousand elsewhere.*
>
> Psalm 84:1–2, 10

Oh, how I long for home. Raising a family would be great, yet I know my heart won't be truly satisfied until I'm standing in the presence of my precious Lord Jehovah. *Come quickly, Lord Jesus!* My dream of heaven is different than the other two, because there is nothing I can do to earn this one, and this one is already guaranteed to me. It was God who sought me and saved me and gave me the promise of heaven.

Heaven is my biggest motivator to live a pure life, simply because when I set my eyes on God's kingdom, the sinful things of earth seem so much less appealing. Our Lord told us to "seek ye first the kingdom of God" (Matthew 6:33 KJV). As songwriter Helen Lemmel noted, when we turn our eyes on Jesus who reigns on high, "the things of earth will grow strangely dim [they'll fade away!] in the light of His glory and grace."[1] Setting our minds on the kingdom of God breaks the very will to sin at its root!

Besides that, heaven motivates me because I want my Lord Jesus to be pleased with me when I enter His place. Near the end of his life, Paul wrote to Timothy, "I have fought the good fight, I have finished the race, I have kept the faith. Now there is in store for me the crown of righteousness, which the Lord, the righteous Judge, will award to me on that day—and not only to me, but also to all who have longed for his appearing" (2 Timothy 4:7–8). Wouldn't you like to be able to say those same words before you die, brother?

Today!

One lie from Satan has tricked most men out there: Single guys cannot live lives of sexual purity. The trend among men in America amplifies that lie. But here's the truth: We do not have to wait until we're married to get our sexual desires under control! It's not just about preparing for our future as husbands and fathers; it's also about living to our full potential in Christ *today!*

Please don't buy into the lie that singleness is a rule-free time of experimentation. Those experiments can cost you your dreams or even your life! Please commit your sexual life to the Lord today.

The battle has caused us too much pain, and we've caused others too much pain as well. Today is a day for victory. If God has broken us for our sins, the time for mourning is coming to an end, and the time for rejoicing is upon us. Let's live pure and holy lives, consecrated and set apart so our heavenly Father can use us more than we ever dreamed. God is moving, guys. He's asking who will join Him. Will we follow our Father, or will we indulge our flesh? We can do only one—we've got to make a choice.

If sexual immorality has a grasp over your mind, your heart, or your life, then please make the decisions described in this book and act on those Scriptures *today!* Your effectiveness for Jesus Christ and for furthering His kingdom will become more than you could have ever imagined, and your walk with Him and your joy in Him will become sweeter than you ever dreamed possible.

REFLECTIONS

1. *What do you look forward to as a result of the new life of purity that the Lord can give you? Make four lists: (a) all the consequences that sexual sin has already cost you; (b) all that sexual sin could cost you if you continue in it; (c) all the blessings that you have already experienced through the times you walked in purity; and (d) all the blessings you look forward to that will be made possible if you heed these lessons and live a life of purity and holiness.*

2. *Look at each list. Which life do you really want to live? Then live it!*

3. *What passions and calling has the Lord laid on your heart that you can pour yourself into wholeheartedly today as a single person, whether you are courting/dating someone or not, that would enable you to seize these blessed days God has gifted you with?*

4. *Go back through the chapters and follow through with anything that you thought you should have done and you put off. Follow through with this today!*

One Giant Prerequisite For Purity

DEAR FRIEND, I have no idea where you are on your walk with God. I'm confident that many reading this book are true children of God and are looking to grow closer to the Lord in the area of sexual purity. But chances are a number of others who call themselves Christians haven't truly repented of their sins and believed in the Lord Jesus with a genuine faith (James 2:14–26). Is that you? Have you been truly born again (John 3:3)?

One popular teaching in the church today says one should never question these things once he's prayed a prayer and thinks he's saved. But the Bible is full of passages that tell us just the opposite: Matthew 25:31–46, Hebrews 12:14, Ephesians 5:5, and Luke 18:17 are just a few.

Hear me clearly: I'm not teaching that a saved person can lose his salvation (John 6:37–40); I'm only teaching that there are clearly many people who've made a profession of faith but are not saved (Matthew 7:21–23).

Oswald Chambers said, "The purity which God demands is impossible unless I can be remade within, and that is what Jesus has undertaken to do by His Redemption."

If you do not have the power of God in your life, none of the things in this book will work for you. Each may help, and you may see some temporary changes in your life as you apply the practical ideas that have worked for many of us, but you will fall back into the same things again and again; you will not be truly changed without God's power. The prerequisite for sexual purity is the power of Christ within.

If you would like to know more about what it is to truly be a born-again believer in Jesus, please read John and Romans in the Bible, and the book *An Anchor for the Soul,* by Ray Pritchard.[1] For more information on spiritual salvation, call 1-800-NEEDHIM to talk with someone about what real spiritual faith is.

❝ While the rule of chastity is the same for all Christians at all times, the rule of propriety changes. When people break the rule of propriety current in the time and place, if they do so in order to excite lust in themselves or others, then they are offending against chastity.

C. S. LEWIS
Mere Christianity

Daughters of Jerusalem, I charge you: do not arouse or awaken love until it so desires. . . . For love is as strong as death, its jealousy unyielding as the grave. It burns like blazing fire, like the very flame of the LORD. Many waters cannot quench love.

Song of Solomon 8:4, 6–7

For Women Only

THE MAIN readers of *Sex and the Single Guy* should be obvious—single guys like me—but I suspect others will read the book as well. I know that a lot of women are going to be curious about what guys are up to, so they will pick up a copy. You may be one of them. So it is to you, my sister in Christ, that I address this "postscript" to the book.

Hi! How's it going? Pretty wild stuff in there, huh? Well, you asked for it by picking up a book by and for the gender that many girls once regarded as having "cooties." (By the way, those cooties never go away; when we get older, they just become annoying back hair.)

Let me share my heart about these issues, as well as the

hearts of many of our brothers in Christ. First of all, thank you for being bold enough to read this book.

I'll put your mind at ease: We're not going to harp on wearing more modest clothing. On that issue I will only acknowledge that dress *was* the biggest thing that the majority of the guys wanted to talk to you about, so please take that seriously. It's true that the guys have to do their part, and that there will always be other scantily clad girls out there, but you really do us a huge favor when you dress modestly. For those of you who do make a point of wearing clothes that will not attract our attention to your body: On behalf of all of our brothers in Christ and myself, *thank you*. That is all I'll say about modesty.

You've probably read some things that have surprised or even shocked you. It may have been alarming to learn that just about every guy you've ever met struggles or has struggled with masturbation. You've learned that many guys have been involved with pornography to some degree. Guys you would have never guessed have. Guys who do these things are not weird psychos. It's not OK, and it's still sin, but be prepared if you find out from your boyfriend someday that even he has struggled or now struggles with these things.

If you find that he does struggle with these things, I ask you to do three things: 1. Give him a copy of this book. 2. Give him a copy of *The Mortification of Sin*. 3. Treat him with the same grace that the Lord Jesus has shown you. If Jesus was willing to forgive him, then shouldn't you as well?

I'm not, however, asking you to let him walk all over you. I'll tell you what I tell my dear younger sister, Janie: If he doesn't treat you like a princess and he doesn't love the Lord Jesus more than you, then he's not good enough for you. Like one sister said in chapter 13, you should never settle. Dr. Neil Clark Warren said, "A bad marriage is a thousand times worse than no marriage at all. . . . If you end up not getting married, it would be so much better than marrying the wrong person"[1] No, sister, don't ever let a guy mistreat you or take advantage of you; you always have the right to end a relationship before you tie the knot.

What I am saying is that *every* guy whom you meet and fall in love with, even the best ones, will have some degree of sexual struggle that you'll have to forgive him for and work through. Our minds work so very different than a girl's does, so please try to understand that in the grace and love of Jesus.

I want you to have the opportunity of hearing from a number of your brothers in Christ, so here you go. All of these are real testimonies from real guys. God bless you as you read, sister, and thank you so much for your partnership in the Gospel.

"Dear Sister," from Your Brother in Christ

"My grandfather told me this once and it has stuck with me. He said, 'Women need to see their bodies as the front of a department store. Don't put on display anything that isn't for sale.' I think all too often, women do not comprehend just how different God has created their minds from ours. I wish they knew and could just for a moment think as we think. Then they would have to become so disgusted with the male gender that they would all become nuns."

"Demand respect and expect us to be men who live as Christ did. Look at each of us as your brothers—look out for me and don't accept anything less than Christ demands."

"I wish that girls knew how powerful their actions really were—the way they dressed, bent over, walked, and their physical touch can all have detrimental results to our minds. For sure, women are not to blame for a man's thought life, but as sisters in Christ, they should be concerned for our welfare and spiritual growth. They need to know that a movie, song, or TV show with sexual content is very difficult for our minds to take in without being negatively influenced. They need to watch out for us, being mindful of the difficulties with this issue. They also need to know that being rid of this struggle is not as easy as 'just stopping' or following a list of practical advice."

"Guys are not perverts (well, not all of them). Very godly men struggle in this area; please be patient with us in our failures. Of course don't encourage temptation, whatever that means for whatever circumstance. We want to be the right kind of men to lead a family and home and marriage, but we are bound to our flesh. As long as we are alive, we will be tempted. Pray for us, and please, please be patient in love."

Notes

Chapter 1: From One Guy to Another

1. John Eldredge, *Wild at Heart* (Nashville: Nelson, 2001), 163.
2. Illustration taken from Mark Irving, Cedarville University youth conference, Cedarville, Ohio, fall 2002.

Chapter 4: Broken and Made Whole

1. Stephen Arterburn, Fred Stoeker, and Mike Yorkey, *Every Young Man's Battle* (Colorado Springs: Waterbrook, 2002), 110–13.
2. Ibid., 110.
3. Julia H. Johnston, "Grace Greater Than Our Sin." Public domain.
4. Taken from a chapel message by Bill Brown, Cedarville University, 24 November 2003.

Chapter 5: How a Warrior Prepares

1. Robert Daniels, *The War Within* (Wheaton, Ill.: Crossway, 1997), 73.

2. In addition to 2 Corinthians 10:5, two other Scriptures that I have memorized and quote often are Job 31:1 and 2 Timothy 2:22, which in the New Living Translation reads, "Run from anything that stimulates youthful lust."

Chapter 7: Lust: Where the Battle Starts

1. D. L. Moody, *The Faith That Overcomes* (London: Morgan, n.d.); as quoted in Steve Miller, *D. L. Moody on Spiritual Leadership* (Chicago: Moody, 2004), 156.

Chapter 8: Pornography: You Can Break Free

1. This is a pamphlet, and no writer is listed.

2. John Eldredge, *Wide at Heart* (Nashville: Nelson, 2001), 187.

3. The fee for the program in 2004 was about $7 a month, or $75 for an annual subscription. For more information, go to the Web site www.covenanteyes.com.

Chapter 9: Masturbation: Unmasking the Lie

1. John Eldredge, *Wild at Heart* (Nashville: Nelson, 2001), 146.

2. Mark Laaser, "Man and Sex: Moving Beyond Selfishness," New Man Weekly Spiritual Booster, a weekly e-mail of *New Man* magazine, 27 February 2004.

3. The study, conducted by Christian Community, Inc., surveyed "religious" teens, those who indicated their faith "is very important or important" to them and are "very involved" in congregational life. In "Faith Matters: Teenagers, Sexuality, and Religion," Steve Clapp, Kristen Leverton Helbert, and Angela Zizak; as reported by the Religious Institute on Sexual Morality, Justice, and Healing; http://www.religiousinstitute.org/matters.html.

Chapter 10: Treat Her Right

1. Randy Pope, *Finding Your Million Dollar Mate* (Chicago: Northfield, 2002), 114.

Chapter 11: A Band of Brothers

1. Robert McGee, *The Search for Significance* (Nashville: W Publishing, 2003), 5; emphasis added.

2. For a list of great books to go through with your mentor, see "For Further Reading," page 219.

Chapter 14: A Deeper Pain

1. Rebecca St. James, *Wait for Me* (Nashville: Nelson, 2002), 70.

2. The survey found that "31 percent of the 11th and 12th grade females surveyed said they have had an [unwanted sexual] experience." In "Faith Matters: Teenagers, Sexuality, and Religion," Steve Clapp, Kristen Leverton Helbert, and Angela Zizak; as reported by the Religious Institute on Sexual Morality, Justice, and Healing; http://www.religiousinstitute.org/matters.html.

Chapter 15: What Life Do You Want?

1. Helen H. Lemmel, "Turn Your Eyes Upon Jesus." Public domain.

Epilogue: One Giant Prerequisite for Purity

1. Ray Pritchard, *An Anchor for the Soul* (Chicago: Moody, 2000). Available through Amazon and other online sites or at your local bookstore.

Afterword: For Women Only

1. Neil Clark Warren, *How to Know If Someone Is Worth Pursuing in Two Dates or Less* (Nashville: Nelson, 2000), 182.

For Further Reading

Finding Fulfillment and Identity in Christ

John Eldridge, *Wild at Heart*. Nashville: Nelson, 2001.

Robert S. McGee, *The Search for Significance*. Nashville: W Publishing, 2003.

Rick Warren, *The Purpose-Driven Life*. Grand Rapids: Zondervan, 2002.

Sexual Purity

Elisabeth Elliot, *Passion and Purity*. Grand Rapids: Revell, 2002.

Robert Daniels, *The War Within*. Wheaton, Ill.: Crossway, 1997.

Bob Gresh, *Who Moved the Goalpost?* Chicago: Moody, 2001.

John Owen, *The Mortification of Sin*. Edinburgh, Scotland: Banner of truth, 2004.

Dating and Romance

Alistair Begg, *Lasting Love*. Chicago: Moody, 1997.

Joshua Harris, *Boy Meets Girl*. Sisters, Oreg.: Multnomah, 2000.

Tommy Nelson, *The Book of Romance*. Nashville: Nelson, 1998.

Randy Pope, *Finding Your Million Dollar Mate*. Chicago: Northfield, 2002.

Neil Clark Warren, *How to Know If Someone Is Worth Pursuing in Two Dates or Less*. Nashville: Nelson, 2000.

SINCE 1894, Moody Publishers has been dedicated to equip and motivate people to advance the cause of Christ by publishing evangelical Christian literature and other media for all ages, around the world. Because we are a ministry of the Moody Bible Institute of Chicago, a portion of the proceeds from the sale of this book go to train the next generation of Christian leaders.

If we may serve you in any way in your spiritual journey toward understanding Christ and the Christian life, please contact us at www.moodypublishers.com.

"All Scripture is God-breathed and is useful for teaching, rebuking, correcting and training in righteousness, so that the man of God may be thoroughly equipped for every good work."
—2 TIMOTHY 3:16, 17

MOODY
PUBLISHERS

THE NAME YOU CAN TRUST®

SEX AND THE SINGLE GUY TEAM

ACQUIRING EDITOR
Greg Thornton

BACK COVER COPY
Elizabeth Cody Newenhuyse

COPY EDITOR
Jim Vincent

COVER DESIGN
The DesignWorks Group, John Hamilton
www.designworksgroup.com

COVER PHOTO
Julian Boss/Photonica

INTERIOR DESIGN
BlueFrog Design

PRINTING AND BINDING
Bethany Press International

The typeface for the text of this book is
RotisSerif

e *was tempted,*
eing tempted.

; youthful lust.
int to do right.
y the companionship
pure hearts.

We take captive every thought *to make it obedient to Christ.*
—2 Corinthians 10:5

*12*So, if you think you are standing firm, *be careful that you don't fall!* *13*No temptation has seized you except what is common to man. And God is faithful; he will not let you be tempted beyond what you can bear. But when you are tempted, he will also **provide a way out** so that you can STAND UP under it.
—1 Corinthians 10:12–13

How can a young man keep his way pure?
By living according to your word.
—Psalm 119:9

Thy word have I hid in mine heart,
that I might not sin against thee.
—Psalm 119:11 KJV

*18*FLEE from sexual immorality. *All other sins a man commits are out-side his body, but he who sins sexually sins against his own body.* *19*Do you not know that your body is a temple of the Holy Spirit, *who is in you, whom you have received from God?* YOU ARE NOT YOUR OWN; *20you were bought at a price. Therefore* honor God with your body.
—1 Corinthians 6:18–20

I made a covenant with my eyes
not to look lustfully at a girl.
—Job 31:1

RUN from anything that
stimulates youthful lust.
—2 Timothy 2:22 NLT

My Battle Plan

Where and When
I'm Most Tempted

1. _____

2. _____

3. _____

What I Can Do
to Gain Victory

1. _____   _____

2. _____   _____

3. _____   _____

4. _____   _____

5. _____

6. _____

Y 241.66 KNABLE
Knable, Joseph.
Sex and the single guy
:winning your battle for

*F   ty
*The 1   · Issue